A CHILD'S TOUCHSTONE

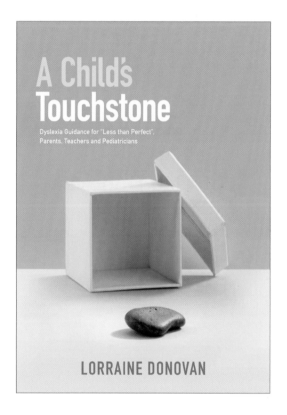

Dyslexia Guidance for "Less than Perfect",
Parents, Teachers and Pediatricians

A Child's Touchstone

Dyslexia Guidance for "Less than Perfect",
Parents, Teachers and Pediatricians

Lorraine Donovan

FRESH
Voice
Publishing

A Child's Touchstone

A CHILD'S TOUCHSTONE
Dyslexia Guidance for "Less than Perfect" Parents, Teachers and Pediatricians
www.achildstouchstone.com

Published by Fresh Voice Publishing
12711 Newport Avenue #C
Tustin, CA 92780
www.freshvoicepublishing.com

Printed in the United States of America
Hardcover, Full Color

ISBN 978-0-9965570-0-9

Copyediting by All My Best, Lynette Smith
Book Cover and Interior Layout Design by Nathan Whitman
Book Cover and Interior Artwork Photography by Jack Fritze Photography
Lorraine Donovan's Portraits by Barbara Higgins Photography
Location for Lorraine Donovan's Photo Shoot provided by
Ethan Allen (Showroom) located in Tustin, California
Awesome Artwork provided by Children with Dyslexia

For my son, Brandon,
<u>who</u> inspired me to write

A Child's Touchstone

Acknowledgements

So many people supported and encouraged me while I was writing *A Child's Touchstone*. I feel incredibly blessed to have such a wonderful circle of family, friends, business clients and colleagues, special education specialists, medical professionals, and teachers who provided me with their valuable insights. I also feel privileged to have met hundreds of parents who shared with me their experiences and challenges in helping their dyslexic child. Thank you for your insight, knowledge and incredible passion for what you do, every day.

A big thank you to all the children who submitted artwork for my book and website (www.achildstouchstone.com). You are amazing artists. Dyslexics rock!

Writing *A Child's Touchstone* has been an incredible journey. My gift to you is to share everything I have learned on dyslexia and how we can make significant positive differences for children with dyslexia. My hope is that this book will start a magnificent wave of new conversations and ideas, generate new understanding and begin a new movement in raising awareness.

And for my son, Brandon, thank you for hanging in there, even when I wasn't sure what I was doing. I love you.

Touchstone

"An excellent quality or example that is
used to test the excellence
or geniuses of others"

Genius

"The guiding spirit who attends a person
from birth to death"

Contents

"Coming together is a beginning.
Keeping together is progress.
Working together is success."

- Henry Ford, Founder of
the Ford Motor Company

List of Forms and Sample Letters

"My mother was the most beautiful woman I ever saw. All I am I owe to my mother. I attribute all my success in life to the moral, intellectual and physical education I received from her."

- George Washington,
1st President of the United States of America

Brandon age 9

"Surround yourself with the dreamers
and doers, the believers and thinkers,
but most of all, surround yourself with
those who see greatness within you,
even when you don't see it yourself."

-Steve Jobs
Co-founder of Apple Inc.

Introduction

Full disclosure – I'm not perfect. In fact, some of my many attributes contain words such as disagreeable, challenging, non-conforming, and ridiculously optimistic. I also happen to be dyslexic, and so is my son. There, I said it—dyslexia.

One of the biggest challenges that dyslexics face is accepting they're dyslexic and owning it! This is because they lack understanding as to how their magnificent dyslexic brain works while learning new information. But once they do, miracles begin to happen.

Being diagnosed with dyslexia can seem confusing and overwhelming but also a relief that unanswered thoughts and questions are finally answered. Knowing is growing.

It's never too early or too late to discover that dyslexia is part of the family gene pool. Sometimes it can even explain some past family member mysteries, such as why Grandpa never read books but always seemed to know so much, or why you or your child has difficulty remembering seemingly simple instructions.

Being dyslexic is really okay. We just need to educate those who affect our daily lives, such as parents, family, friends and teachers that dyslexia is real, and for millions of people, a blessing in disguise.

The fact you're holding this book in your hands says you're ready to learn what dyslexia is all about. And you made the right decision. This book gives you a significant "jumpstart" in learning everything you need to know about dyslexia, how children with dyslexia get help, and how you and others are part of the solution.

You'll be pleased to know that nothing in this book is clinical or boring. Readers appreciate simplicity and inspiration while learning.

In the next few pages, you'll be guided by instructions on reading *A Child's Touchstone*. It is important to work through the learning process, step by step. And although you'll be tempted to jump ahead, have patience by starting in the beginning.

Be prepared however, to experience all kinds of feelings, including epiphanies and a renewed awareness on dyslexia.

Let's get started. Turn the page.

"Most of the important things in the world have been accomplished by people who have kept on trying when there seemed to be no hope at all."

- Dale Carnegie,
American writer and lecturer

Michael age 12

"The time is ripe, and rotten-ripe,
for change. Then let it come."

-James Russell Lowell
American romantic poet

Past and Present

When I was a little girl, life seemed much less complicated. Children spent most of their daily lives outside, playing with neighbor kids, creating imaginary adventures in their innocent world.

School was welcoming and relatively stress free. Teachers were highly respected (parents saw to that) and children responded with "please" and "thank you." Adoration between student and teacher were commonplace, as was the school's relationship with the local community.

I remember how natural it was for teachers to stay after school to help struggling students, with no forethought to the time it was taking. And although dyslexia was not generally known about, I never felt different, even when it was I who needed the extra help.

But things change and we're supposed to change with it. Along the way however, things went askew.

Years have passed, and the process for identifying children with such specific learning disabilities as dyslexia has made little progress. Mounds of paperwork and long waiting times, before and after evaluation, have become the norm. School evaluators and educators lack knowledgeable training on dyslexia and often misdiagnose, and the needs of students with dyslexia still go unattended.

Teachers who think they're teaching students with disabilities correctly are now lacking training across the board. Laws are changing faster than educators can keep up with, an unfortunate combination and a recipe for disaster. The word "dyslexia" has become a dirty word and is rarely acknowledged in academic environments.

Instead, schools and teachers are feverishly preoccupied with implementing other types of learning disability supports that do not include students with dyslexia. After all, they think dyslexic students seem intelligent but are just lacking in motivation.

Such beliefs transcend dyslexia as "not being that big a deal," because, in their eyes, dyslexic students do not seem academically disabled. Sadly, ignorance ("willful blindness") of dyslexia dominates the field of education because most educators are ill-equipped and untrained to teach in the specific ways dyslexic students learn.

Doing the same thing and expecting different results has never helped children with dyslexia and never will. And the voices of worried parents and teachers resonate this fact.

Children with dyslexia have tremendous abilities and talents and deserve to be taught in ways they learn, and not the other way around.

It's time for a new action plan, one that includes more kinesthetic learning, out-of-the-box thinking, one-on-one teaching and much less paperwork.

Take comfort in knowing that while *A Child's Touchstone* was being written, no stone was left unturned; every area of the life of the dyslexic child is covered.

So we begin—to change society's perception on dyslexia, and to help children in ways we never imagined possible.

PS. Don't give up: The beginning is always the hardest.

Matthew age 14

"The sky's the limit. Success is not limited.
You need to recognize that you can never
learn too much. The opportunities are always
there, just waiting to be grasped. There are
stars whose radiance are still visible on Earth,
even though they have long been extinct."

-Anonymous

Feelings

Discovering your child has a learning disability isn't always welcome news. Parents, especially, have difficulties accepting that their child is struggling academically due to dyslexia.

Some parents go into denial, blaming the teacher's lack of attention as the reason their child is struggling in school. On the flip side, some teachers blame parents for their lack of involvement in their child's academic experience. In so blaming, both parents and teachers are wrong and solve nothing.

Most parents and teachers are 100% committed to the academic success of their children and students. Why then, do some well intentioned parents and teachers get wrapped up in unproductive emotions and paralyzed by denial, blame, fear, envy, anger and guilt? It's because none of us are perfect.

Imagine running away from something that keeps pace with your flight. Exhaustion and resentment are not far behind, and they will continue to build momentum until dealt with. Translate this to how some parents react to learning their child has a learning disability; their whole world is falling apart.

Everyone experiences life's challenges differently. One thing is sure though: The more knowledge and understanding of the issue, the less stress and fear take over.

Since you're reading this, you are taking the first steps in conquering your fears, stress and anxiety. Please know that everything is going to be okay: A dyslexic child is counting on you.

Marabelle age 11

"Children are likely to live up to
what you believe in them."

-Lady Bird Johnson (1912-2007)
First Lady of the United States, 1963-1969

A Message to Parents

No one is going to tell you what to do, but if you're willing to take some advice, you've come to the right place. Trust me when I tell you I've been where you are today.

Nothing is more overwhelming than news your child has a learning disability. For those bringing the news, it's a matter of fact. For you, it's an emergency.

Racing, unfamiliar thoughts consume every breath as you try to sort out what to do, yet nothing comes to mind. You're looking for an action plan and assume there is one… somewhere.

The truth is, if you're relying on most schools, teachers, special education specialists or others to have all the answers, you'll be greatly disappointed. It's up to those closest to the dyslexic child to actively seek answers to all unanswered questions. This includes educating yourself on dyslexia and how to help your child succeed academically. It isn't easy, but it's certainly worth it.

Understanding dyslexia takes knowledge and time. The good news is that *A Child's Touchstone* gives you a five year jumpstart on everything you need to know.

Read this book from the beginning and don't skip over anything. Don't let anyone diminish your concern or defeat your purpose. Reach out for help from those willing to give it. Believe in yourself, and be the change you want to see.

Try not to worry too much; I'm right here with you!

Jeffrey age 15

"In education it isn't how much you have committed to memory or even how much you know. It's being able to differentiate between what you do know and what you don't. It's knowing where to go to find out what you need to know and it's knowing how to use the information you get."

-William Feather
American publisher and author

A Message to Teachers

I know what you may be thinking: Another boring book on dyslexia, full of scientific data and goal requirements, and lacking in hands-on applications that really work in the classroom. Nope!

Classroom teachers are the academic glue that binds the book of knowledge. Without teachers, no student would have the opportunity to know and learn what teachers offer and how their teachings translate into lifelong success. It is important for classroom teachers to be heard and supported; that's why this book takes teachers to a new level of learning and teaching.

Choosing to learn about dyslexia is a professional choice. If you're reading this, something has caught your attention. Are you concerned about a dyslexic student in your classroom? Does a parent believe you can help their child, when no one else can? Is awareness about dyslexia elevating your interest?

Whatever is driving you to learn more, go with it! Let your "gut feeling" be your guide. Remember, you are a professional educator, with independent thoughts and ethics. Think "student first." Be that "special teacher" we all talk about.

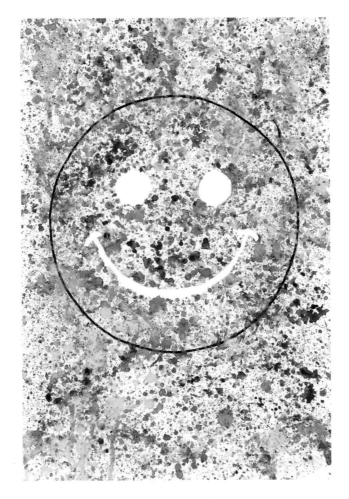

James age 10

"There are only two things a child will share willingly: communicable diseases and his mother's age."

-Benjamin Spock, (1903-1998)
American pediatrician and author

A Message to Pediatricians

Let's face it. A 15 minute doctor visit isn't enough time to determine whether a patient has a learning disability. Most visits don't include in-depth questioning of the patient's academic performance.

Well intentioned pediatricians rely too heavily on their patients' parents to freely offer up accurate information of potential academic struggles. Most parents, however, cannot reconcile what that means.

Medical questionnaires aren't much better. A lot of parents are uncomfortable completing lengthy forms on their child's learning and developmental abilities.

The solution requires a delicate balance of knowledge on learning disabilities and a persistence to question further.

It isn't easy. No one wants to hear their child needs further evaluation for a possible learning disability. But if pediatricians won't take the lead, who will?

Pediatricians are a child's first line of defense. Being knowledgeable on learning disabilities can save a child from a lifetime of undue suffering.

Pediatricians should read this book, using it as a guide and referral for further evaluation. It's also a great resource for parents who wish to learn more about dyslexia and how to help their child.

Hailey age 9

"Genius is neither learned nor acquired. It is knowing without experience. It is risking without fear of failure. It is perception without touch. It is understanding without research. It is certainty without proof. It is ability without practice. It is invention without limitations. It is imagination without boundaries. It is creativity without constraints. It is...extraordinary intelligence!"

-Patricia Polacco,
Author of children's books

A Child's Touchstone

No one knows how many of the world's population are dyslexic, but the numbers are in the millions.

Current data suggests 15 to 20% of the population have a learning disability, and 85% of them are dyslexic. This means if there are 30 students in a classroom, 4 to 5 have dyslexia. And for each child identified with dyslexia, 3 are missed. In fact, less than one-third of students with reading disabilities are receiving additional educational services that they so desperately need.

We know dyslexics are highly creative, out-of-the-box thinkers with the ability to learn and see things differently, yet they rarely receive the academic support or understanding from those who know them best.

To gain perspective of the impact people with dyslexia have on society, we simply need to look around us. Many well known leaders, scientists, artists, poets, actors, inventors, architects, entrepreneurs and other like-minded people have dyslexia.

It's no coincidence that genius exists with dyslexics. The great architects and builders of the Pyramids of Egypt and coliseums of the Roman Empire are examples of genius, when most people in the world were non-readers and non-writers.

It wasn't until the eighteenth century that reading for knowledge began changing how people learn. "Learning by doing" was being replaced with "learning by reading." For people with dyslexia however, their hands-on style of learning was being replaced with written words.

Fast forward to today, and not much has changed. Children with dyslexia are still being required to learn in ways that don't match their learning style, even when there is scientific evidence proving the long-term negative effects of these teaching methods. And yet, with all the in-depth research, dyslexia is still the most misunderstood learning style among school-aged children.

Is it because we can't "see" dyslexia (unlike other disabilities) and therefore don't believe it exists? Tell that to a germ. Perhaps it's because dyslexia is not seen as that serious; tell that to a struggling third grader who hates school because he can't read very well.

It's time for new conversations, new ideas and renewed awareness on dyslexia, because the old ones aren't getting through anymore. *A Child's Touchstone*, Dyslexia Guidance for "Less than Perfect" Parents, Teachers and Pediatricians, does just that, and much, much more!

So join me, while learning how dyslexics think, learn and flourish.

Elizabeth age 13

"Always be a first-rate version
of yourself, instead of a second-
rate version of somebody else."

-Judy Garland, Singer and Actress

Uncomplicating the Complicated

I never felt more confused, overwhelmed and alone than when I began researching dyslexia to help my son. Determining how and where to look wasn't as easy as I thought. There were no direct instructions or guidance offered, no medical insurance support, no teacher understanding of dyslexia, and no money for sending my son to private school for dyslexics. At that point, I knew it was up to me to find the answers and advocate for my son's rights to his learning style.

In the beginning, it was hard. Concerns for my son's academic needs did not seem as important to those responsible for his learning. I was listened to, but there was no follow-through. I felt placated by administrators who were more concerned about how it was going to affect them, than by how anything was going to help my son. And the more I learned about dyslexia, the more the ignorance of others surrounded me.

Relationships with my son's teachers changed as well. In their eyes, I went from being the dutiful, volunteer-for-everything parent to one who expected them to teach to my son's dyslexia learning style—which they neither knew nor wanted to learn. It was exhausting.

As time passed and my knowledge grew, so did my determination. The status quo was no longer acceptable. Taking a stand made the difference, and how I began to write *A Child's Touchstone.*

Special education policies have become so convoluted and complicated that even those charged with implementation question their outcomes. Teachers lack knowledge and training on dyslexia and rely completely on special education staff for all the answers and support—obviously a failing policy. And parents are left to fend for themselves.

Teaching in ways a dyslexic child learns is not that complicated. Poor educational policies are what complicate educational support. No dyslexic child should have to wait several months or years before receiving educational supports, all because failing policies and inadequate procedures trump awaiting academic support for a struggling student.

I wrote *A Child's Touchstone* to help parents, teachers and pediatricians understand dyslexia and the dyslexic, in an uncomplicated way.

Let's get started.

Aaron age 15

"I think, at a child's birth, if a mother could ask a fairy godmother to endow it with the most useful gift, that gift would be curiosity."

-Eleanor Roosevelt
U.S. First Lady, 1933 to1945

CHAPTER 1

Getting to Know a Dyslexic

No matter what anyone says or thinks, you can't change how dyslexics learn. To try is futile.

Dyslexics are global learners. They learn best when information is introduced to them through storytelling, current events or personal experience, colorful illustration, visual movement, music, humor and active hands-on participation.

Insisting on trying to make dyslexics learn the way 80% of the population learns is a mistake. Give up now and accept this fact.

Embracing a dyslexic's learning style can be very rewarding for teachers, parents and society. The newness and willingness to understand dyslexia can be incredibly satisfying. Just talk with someone who has taken steps to learn about dyslexia and your perspective will definitely change—for the better.

Dyslexics have the best ideas….on most everything! Maybe it's because dyslexics tend to think in pictures, prefer to identify the goal and work upwards to the end result and rarely accept "It isn't possible" as the answer. "Why not?" is more likely.

To fully understand dyslexics, it's important to know all their wonderful traits. And though 80% of the world's population are non-dyslexic, the 20% who are provide the necessary balance. All that's needed is time to mature, from childhood to adulthood, without the ignorance of some, and with support from those who are closest to them.

Embracing a dyslexic's qualities is easy. But before doing so, you may need to first dismiss some or all preconceived understanding on dyslexia. With that done, read on and be enlightened......

- Not a jealous bone in their body. Dyslexics are first to recognize and celebrate the successes of others. If you don't believe me, just watch how they light up with smiles of happiness when you tell them about the accomplishment of another.

- Gentle and kind to all life's creatures. Dyslexics are famous for defending the less fortunate or most vulnerable, including a praying mantis in danger of being amputated by a not-so-compassionate child.

- Generous heart and pocketbook. Dyslexic children are first to offer to share their lunch or snack with a seemingly hungry classmate, and if they have a dollar, are first give to help feed another. Dyslexic children are sensitive to the needs of others. (Are you crying yet?)

- Forgiving. Dyslexic children are often bullied by their peers (even by some teachers and parents) yet are incredibly forgiving. They believe everyone deserves another chance, and they're willing to forgive and forget, even while others still hold grudges.

- Friendly spirit. Dyslexics are not mean—to anyone. Bullies (of all ages and position) are mean and demeaning. Dyslexics are not. It is not in their DNA.

- Honest communication. Dyslexic children speak the truth by what they see and hear. Unlike their weakness in reading, their sense of seeing and hearing are strong and dominate their conscience.

- Visually and spatially observant. Think of the child who suggests the tires be deflated in order to move the stuck truck. Dyslexics have the incredible ability to visualize the end result by looking at the whole picture.

- Creative problem solving. Tell a dyslexic you need their help in solving a problem and you'll receive the best result. Dyslexics process information differently and embrace new ideas easily, which means problem-solving outcomes are brilliant and fantastic.

- Great imagination. Ask daydreaming dyslexics what they're thinking about, and most will say "nothing," when in fact, they're doing the opposite.

- Strong sense of fairness. Dyslexic children know what it means to not be treated fairly and are first to offer support and balance to the underserved. Surprisingly, their desire for fairness comes from their strength of what is least given to them.

- Vivid imagination and creativity. It isn't uncommon for dyslexic children to become great artists, actors, chefs, architects, teachers, engineers, scientists, psychologists, designers, photographers, musicians, athletes and even public speakers. All of these professions require a lively imagination and uninhibited creativity. No problem for the dyslexic.

- Intense curiosity. Dyslexic children are incredibly curious and enjoy the complexity of seeing things differently. This sparks further interest in thinking and perceiving what they learn multi-dimensionally by deliberately and intentionally using all senses to engage curiosity.

- Excellent listening skills. In one-on-one interactions with dyslexics, no one else can match their listening skills. Not only will they listen intently, but they'll show genuine interest in what is being shared by the other person. This is a wonderful quality to have.

- Enthusiastically step up and offer help. Dyslexic children naturally like to help out, whether in the classroom, at a senior center, during summer camp or in a soup kitchen. Just ask them and watch the magic happen.

- Trustworthy. Entrust your last dollar with a dyslexic and you're in good hands.

- Non-judgmental. Out-of-the-box thinkers do not judge others. Instead, they offer simple suggestions.

- Exceptionally observant. Dyslexics notice things that others don't, such as, "Why didn't the teacher smile when I got part of the answer correct?"

- Self-determined. Dyslexics already know the big picture and will get there in their own way.

- Make the best, best friends...

"Children have a remarkable talent for not taking the adult world with the kind of respect we are so confident it ought to be given. To the irritation of authority figures of all sorts, children expend considerable energy in "clowning around." They refuse to appreciate the gravity of our monumental concerns, while we forget that if we were to become more like children our concerns might not be so monumental".

- Conrad Hyers (1933-2013),
American writer

Bryant age 13

"You can know the name of a bird in all the
languages of the world, but when you're finished,
you'll know absolutely nothing whatever about
the bird... So let's look at the bird and see what
its' doing -- that's what counts. I learned very
early the difference between knowing the
name of something and knowing something."

-Richard Feynman, American physicist

CHAPTER 2

Myths and Misconceptions

Important as it is to know what dyslexia is, it is just as important to know what it is <u>not</u>. Below is a list of some of those myths and misconceptions:

- Dyslexics develop brain pathways at a slower pace than non dyslexics—false. A dyslexic's processing styles are just developing in a different way. The dyslexic's brain creates different processing patterns for connections, circuitry and problem solving. These differences in processing patterns are constructively global, complete and strong. These differences are not weaknesses—they're just different.

- Everyone is a little dyslexic and they outgrow it—false. Dyslexia is a life long condition. There is no cure. One in five people (of those evaluated) have dyslexia.

- Dyslexia affects mostly poor people—false. Dyslexia exists in all cultures and across all ranges of abilities and socio-economic backgrounds. Dyslexia does not discriminate and exists worldwide.

- Dyslexia skips generations—false. If one parent has dyslexia, there is a 50% chance that one or all of their offspring will also have dyslexia.

- Dyslexia is an intellectual disability—false. Dyslexia does not affect intelligence/I.Q. Dyslexics have a different learning preference, not a low ability to learn.

- Dyslexics read words/or letters backwards—false. Dyslexics do not see words or letters backwards (or mirror writing). Dyslexics may reverse b with d, which is caused by confusion over left versus right during decoding of language.

- Retaining (holding back) students with dyslexia will improve academic struggles—false. School retention is a failed educational policy and does not improve academic struggles for dyslexic students.

- Dyslexia is caused by a lack of phonics instruction—false. Dyslexic children given phonics instruction will not know how to apply it. A classic warning sign of dyslexia is a child who cannot sound out an unknown word, despite being taught phonics.

- Dyslexia affects boys more than girls—false.

- Dyslexia cannot be diagnosed until third grade—false. Professionals who conduct cognitive testing can accurately diagnose reading problems in children as young as five years of age.

- Most children outgrow their reading and spelling problems. It's just a temporary glitch—false. Waiting for a child to grow out of it is futile. The child will just continue to fall further and further behind, academically.

- Children with dyslexia are just lazy—false. Society is just impatient.

- Dyslexia only occurs in languages using the alphabet, not in countries with logographic languages like China and Japan—false. Chinese and Japanese students make the same sound based phonological mistakes that English speakers do, or others with alphabetic languages such as Spanish, Italian or French.

- Most teachers, reading specialists and special education teachers are highly trained in dyslexia and its remediation methods—false. Sadly, most teachers, reading specialists and special education teachers/resource specialists have little to no knowledge, training or education related to dyslexia.

- Most classroom teachers know the warning signs of dyslexia, notify the parents and refer the student for evaluation for a learning disability—false. Most teachers have no training in dyslexia and its classic warning signs.

- Only children with an IEP or 504 Plan can receive classroom accommodations—false. Teachers are free to provide classroom accommodations to any student, regardless of whether that student has an IEP or 504 Plan or not. School administrators and/or teachers are misinformed when they use the excuse that they cannot provide accommodations unless a student has an IEP or 504 Plan.

- In order for the dyslexic student to learn how to spell, teacher(s) should mark off and reduce the student's grade for spelling errors—false. A dyslexic child has great difficulty with spelling. Therefore, marking off for spelling errors will not teach him/her how to spell. Schoolwork should be graded on content, not spelling.

- Classroom accommodations are a crutch and just make the dyslexic student dependent and lazy—false. No student would choose to have dyslexia. They do not want to be different from their peers. They would much rather be able to complete assignments the very same way as their peers, but they can't—plain and simple.

- Dyslexia is a catch-all term—false. Dyslexia means "trouble with words," is neurological in origin and is considered a "specific" learning disability. Characteristics include problems accurately and fluently recognizing words, making spelling mistakes and having an inability to decode a word. Reading comprehension issues and a lack of reading experiences are unintended consequences that hinder vocabulary and background knowledge.

- A child who can read, cannot have dyslexia—false. Even children with dyslexia can read in varying degrees. This doesn't mean, however, that dyslexics necessarily comprehend (or remember) what they are reading. Oral reading is misleading as well, because dyslexic children often cannot sound out what they are reading. Instead, they learn to use contextual clues, such as pictures or the familiarity of a story—or they just guess.

- If a child does not qualify for special education services, then he/she does not have dyslexia—false. Schools that do not evaluate for dyslexia are ill-equipped to make that determination.

- Learning disabilities, such as dyslexia, are only academic in nature. They do not affect other areas of a person's life—false. Dyslexia is a lifelong condition. If gone undetected and the student struggles unduly during the school years, then the same learning disabilities that interfere with reading, writing and math can also interfere during adulthood with sports and other activities, family life, social skills and career/employment.

"People travel to wonder at the height of mountains, at the huge waves of the seas, at the long course of the rivers, at the vast compass of the oceans, at the circular motion of the stars, and yet they pass by themselves without wondering."

- Saint Augustine

Katelyn age 5

"A child of five would understand this.
Send someone to fetch a child of five."

-Groucho Marx, Actor
1890-1977

CHAPTER 3

Demystifying Dyslexia and Specific Learning Disabilities

Our education system has done a great job confusing most of us as to what specific learning disabilities are, and how dyslexia is defined. I'll try to describe them as simply as possible, but no guarantee that it won't put you to sleep. Here goes….

There are fourteen distinct disability categories where school-aged children may need additional educational services. They include autism, deaf blindness, deafness, developmental delay, emotional disturbance, hearing impairment, intellectual disability, multiple disabilities, orthopedic impairment, other health impairment, **specific learning disability**, speech or language impairment, traumatic or acquired brain injury and visual impairment.

Within the category of **specific learning disability** are listed four sub-categories of neurological differences/diversities. **Dyslexia** is identified as one of the sub-categories.

The term specific learning disability is described as a disorder in one or more of the basic psychological processes involved in understanding or using language and/or using concepts through verbal or written language. This also includes nonverbal means, such as thinking and listening.

The unintended consequences of having a specific learning disability include deficits in memory, processing of information, reading, writing, spelling, calculation, social competence, emotional maturity, coordination, attention and communication.

The term learning disability is not a specific term; rather, it describes "specific" disabilities, all of which cause learning to be difficult.

Federal law describes specific learning disabilities as disorders that are perceptual disabilities, brain injuries, minimal brain dysfunctions, **dyslexia** or developmental aphasia.

Although most educational specialists/therapists acknowledge dyslexia as a learning disability, school districts get to decide which term to use—"dyslexia" or "specific learning disability"—when determining eligibility for special education services and/or accommodations.

Some school districts prefer to define a learning disability based upon actual identifiable symptoms. For them, the term specific learning disability is too vague when designing an appropriate Individual Education Plan (IEP). If an evaluation identifies dyslexia signs or symptoms, then the child is dyslexic, and a generic term of specific learning disability would not describe this fact.

Others prefer to use the term specific learning disability, and believe the umbrella term covers similar evaluation procedures, educational therapies and support. This is problematic when designing an educational plan for a dyslexic student, as it will, in most cases, lack specific educational therapies and goals that help dyslexic students learn.

As mentioned earlier, there are four sub-categories that describe "specific learning disabilities" and affect eight areas of learning (listening comprehension, oral expression, written expression, basic reading skills, reading fluency, reading comprehension, math calculation and math reasoning/problem solving).

The four sub-categories are:

Dyslexia—difficulties in reading, spelling and writing, due to short-term working memory problems, visual processing problems and/or auditory processing problems. This book covers the rest, in detail.

- Dysgraphia—difficulties with handwriting and putting thoughts on paper. Signs of dysgraphia include:

  - Tight, awkward pen or pencil grip and body position.

  - Avoiding writing.

  - Trouble forming letter writing or printing shapes.

  - Inconsistent spacing between letters or words.

  - Poor understanding of uppercase/lowercase letters.

  - Inability to write or draw in a line or within margins.

  - Tiring quickly while writing.

- Dyspraxia—difficulties in physical motor skills development while learning to write or draw. Signs of dyspraxia include:

  - Difficulty learning to walk, jump and skip.

  - Difficulty pronouncing words and being understood.

  - Difficulty establishing left to right-handedness.

  - Bumping into things frequently.

  - Being easily irritated by touch and clothing on skin.

- Dyscalculia—difficulties in calculating numbers or grasping mathematical concepts. Two major areas of weakness can contribute to math learning disabilities:

  1. Visual spatial difficulties, which result in a student having trouble processing what the eyes see, and/or;

  2. Language processing difficulties, which result in a student having trouble processing and making sense of what the ears hear.

Those with dyscalculia may have difficulty understanding math concepts and solving even simple math problems. Signs of dyscalculia include:

- Difficulty learning to count.

- Difficulty recognizing printed numbers.

- Poor memory for numbers.

- Difficulty organizing things in a logical way.

Are you asleep yet? Oh, good! Almost done. Keep reading…

In addition to the four sub-categories under the heading of specific learning disabilities, the professional medical community (neuropsychologists, clinical psychologists, etc.), has identified these ten sub-types of dyslexia, which they believe are more specific to symptoms of dyslexia:

- Dysnemkinesia (Motor)—poor memory of motor movements involved in writing and printing numbers and letters (including number and letter reversals). Dysgraphia (difficulty with writing) and dyspraxia (difficulty with motor skills), are names synonymous with dysnemkinesia.

- Dysphonesia (Auditory Processing Weakness)—poor at phonetic (sounding out) spelling of words. Dysphonesia is also known as phonological, dysphonetic or auditory dyslexia. Problems with ambient noise, inability to distinguish between sounds that are similar, missing subtle social cues and sensitivity to loud sounds or a dislike for noisy places are common. Weakness in auditory processing is not an issue with hearing sounds; instead, the issue is how the brain interprets what is being heard. A quiet room versus a loud classroom can determine what the child interprets. Inconsistent input of reading instruction makes learning word structure very difficult. Children with auditory processing weakness will often compensate by using their visual strengths as a strategy for learning how to read. They will learn whole words as an image, like memorizing shapes or pictures, rather than trying to decode words.

- Dyseidesia (Visual)—problems with sight word reading (decoding) and spelling (encoding) of words. Students slowly sound out words, spell phonetically, have poor decoding of unfamiliar or unknown words, have difficulty with syllables and have difficulty sounding out and blending the sounds necessary to decode a word. Word substitution (such as home for house) is also common. Dyseidesia is also known as surface dyslexia or visual dyslexia.

- Dysphoneidesia—severe deficits in reading as well as with visual motor integration and working memory.

  - Dysphoneidesia is also known as mixed dyslexia (a combination of dysphonesia (auditory) and dyseidesia (visual).

- Dysnemkinphonesia—a combination of dysnemkinesia (motor) and dysphonesia (auditory).

- Dysnemkineidesia—a combination of dysnemkinesia (motor) and dyseidesia (visual).

- Dysenemkinphoneidesia—a combination of dysnemkinesia (motor), dysphonesia (auditory), and dyseidesia (visual).

- Dysnomia—trouble recalling a word, so they say "the thingy" when they cannot retrieve the word quickly. Dysnomia is also known as semantic dyslexia or naming-speed dyslexia.

- Double deficit—a combination of dysphonesia or phonological dyslexia and dysnomia.

- Dyscalculia—difficulty with mathematics.

Although these sub-categories and sub-types may seem overwhelming, it is important that parents and teachers know they exist, what they mean and how they can hinder a child's ability to learn.

Serena age 15

"There's a crack in everything.
That's how the light gets in."

-Leonard Cohen,
Singer/songwriter

PASS CODE: Genius

CHAPTER 4

Detecting the Symptoms

In a school learning environment, teachers are first to notice signs indicating a different learning preference in a student and share these observations with the parent(s). This practice occurs when teacher(s) have in depth knowledge and training on learning disabilities, their symptoms and how the disability negatively impacts the learning process. But what happens when teachers fail to detect these different learning preferences because they lack the training and knowledge necessary to understand the discrepancy? The student goes undetected and undiagnosed and is left to suffer tremendous academic failure throughout the school years.

Sadly, most kindergarten through twelfth-grade teachers lack the training needed to detect specific learning disabilities such as dyslexia. And although some may have received a few credit hours while acquiring their teaching credential, most agree that it was forgotten shortly afterwards and never brought up again. These facts are indisputable. Waiting for teachers and school administration to be trained on dyslexia is not an option dyslexic children can depend on.

The only way to counter-act the underlying problem is for parents to learn everything possible about dyslexia, how it affects their children and what will help them during their school-age years.

Parents and teachers need to be attuned to the following symptoms that are indicative of dyslexia:

- Difficulty with short-term "working" memory. Dyslexic children's ability to process information in their short-term working memory is compromised, thereby preventing them from holding information long enough to process completely. Working memory refers to the ability to hold on to pieces of information until the pieces blend into a full thought or concept. To read each word until the end of a sentence or paragraph and understand the full content is an example of working memory.

  Short-term memory is the active process of storing and retaining information for a limited period. The information is temporarily available but not yet stored for long-term retention. Short-term and working memory issues result in an inability to recall information such as a lengthy passage from a story they just read (lacking in comprehension/memory issues), being unable to remember important facts on tests, misspelling words, having a weak vocabulary, not remembering the order of operations in mathematics or word problems and much more. Untrained and misinformed teachers believe that memory and organizational problems are under the child's control. They are wrong.

- Difficulty in reading fluidly (smoothly). As a result of short-term memory issues, children with dyslexia often find it difficult to pronounce words correctly, or they miss words completely when reading. Add stress and anxiety to the mix, and dyslexic children may lose their place while reading and even begin stuttering, all the while not remembering anything they may have read aloud in class.

- Organization difficulties. Most dyslexics have difficulty organizing materials and often lose, forget or misplace papers, notebooks or homework assignments. They also have difficulty with school projects that are due at a specific time. Problems with organizing their time or environment are also prevalent, including telling time with an analog clock, as well as becoming misplaced in unfamiliar surroundings.

- Difficulty inferring the meaning of words or concepts. Jokes, idioms or puns are often not understood. Problems occur with words that might have different meanings depending on how they are used, such as "the dog," which refers to a pet, versus "you dog," which suggests an insult.

- Sequencing difficulties. Dyslexics have difficultly organizing thoughts into their proper order, such as the alphabet, months of the year, math order of operations, or multiplication tables. A school assignment may have all the important facts but not be in proper order.

- Avoidance of opportunities for reading, especially aloud in a classroom setting. If gone undiagnosed, dyslexic children will do everything possible to avoid reading aloud. They have already experienced tremendous embarrassment and teasing by their peers. Some teachers even believe that a dyslexic child's seeming lack of effort or attention is the reason for their below average reading level. These types of negative comments only cause the dyslexic child to avoid reading at all, which can then lead to hesitation in speech (fear of speaking improperly).

- Distractibility and oversensitivity to loud sounds and background noise. Dyslexics often show symptoms of overstimulation in their brain's auditory processing cortex. Auditory over-stimulation can occur when there is a weakness in learning to decode language (during the working memory process). When this occurs, their auditory sense becomes stronger in order to compensate for other areas of weakness. Similar compensations occur in those who are blind, where sense of smell or hearing may become more stimulated to compensate for lack of ability to see.

  Most dyslexics exhibit signs of being easily distracted. Some teachers believe these students have difficulty staying on task because they consciously choose to be distracted with other things, and will reprimand them for such behavior. These teachers couldn't be more wrong.

Dyslexics do not choose to be distracted. Their auditory processing is simply over-stimulated, whereby the brain is processing information at a greater frequency, responding to every sound or background noise, unable to ignore or filter out nonsense activity from their surroundings. This interrupts their ability to focus on the tasks required of them in a classroom setting, including difficulty processing and understanding things said when there are competing sounds. Parents and teachers accuse children with dyslexia of having poor attention span and lacking in concentration, but it isn't their fault.

- Difficulty following directions. Again, the dyslexic's working memory is the problem. Without the ability to process all the information into short-term memory, not all information gets relayed or placed in order. Not only do some directions get missed or mixed up, but they can also be confused with subsequent directions received later in the day. Teachers and parents can become easily frustrated because they feel the dyslexic child has complete control over this process and is just being lazy. This is not the case.

- Confusion due to visual crowding/overload. When there is too much information on a page (cramped text, lines, symbols or diagrams), a dyslexic's brain may react to visual crowding. The visual working memory "desk space" is overloaded. They become confused as to what to focus on. This is known as a figure ground problem. They may unintentionally skip words, skip problems on worksheets and tests, skip lines, read the same line twice or show difficulty distinguishing subtle differences in shapes or certain letters or numbers, thus misreading the symbols. Visual overload drains the brain's ability to process information, so reading ability is slow and exhaustive.

Crowding of text, lines, symbols, diagrams and info graphics is overwhelmingly evident in the design layout of most school textbooks. Novels are printed in text sizes so small that even non-dyslexics can have reading fatigue. Visual crowding contributes significantly to slowness in reading words.

And to save cost of paper and printer ink, teachers will cram worksheets or test information onto fewer pages or even onto just one page. These worksheets and tests are quite often recopied over and over again, which ends up distorting or shrinking the text and lightening or smearing the wording, lines and symbols.

- Inability to understand and process the written word due in part to some teachers' poor penmanship. Common penmanship problems include incorrect posture and alignment of letters, mixing printed and cursive letters in the same word, scribbling unidentifiably, miniature style writing and incomplete written words and sentences.

- Difficulty reading and processing information presented by poorly designed school materials, worksheets, textbooks and tests. Dyslexics' ability to process information is dramatically reduced and creates many academic challenges, such as:

  - Difficulty distinguishing between similar forms such as circle vs. oval and square vs. rectangle.

  - Difficulty classifying things; struggling to see similarities and differences.

  - Confusion with order of vowels, such as oa/ao and ou/uo.

  - Difficulty with spatial terms, such as in, out, over, in between, and below.

  - Difficulty looking up places on a map or words in a dictionary.

- Difficulty understanding assignments or tests with double-negative confusion. Tests that contain double-negative questions do not measure the student's level of understanding. Instead, they are meant to trick the reader into thinking the opposite, which has nothing to do with learning the content.

- Difficulty making friends; being socially awkward. A dyslexic child can be extremely social with family and close family friends; however, it can be a different story in a school environment. Being criticized, teased or humiliated (bullied) in the classroom or on the playground is all it takes for the dyslexic child to begin withdrawing socially. Peers learn quickly which students struggle in school, and some teachers do nothing to shield this fact from the rest of the class. Once this information is disclosed, dyslexic students will start avoiding emotional pain by staying quiet and avoiding classroom participation. Their social development skills begin to suffer, as do their self confidence and self esteem.

- Struggling academically and not wanting to attend school. An emotionally safe learning environment is extremely important for dyslexic children. If they do not want to go to school, something is wrong in their school environment. Not feeling successful in school learning will trigger this response. Dyslexic children overwhelmingly feel different when they cannot learn the same way as their peers and their schoolwork reflects red marked corrections and a low grade. And if the teacher does not detect a learning difference preference and continues to teach the same way, the dyslexic student will continue to struggle and fail academically.

- Stress and anxiety. Dyslexics suffer higher levels of stress and anxiety during testing situations, which dramatically reduces their ability to focus. Also prevalent are feelings of being overwhelmed with large amounts of reading or writing.

"Normal day, let me be aware of the treasure you are. Let me learn from you, love you, savor you, bless you before you depart. Let me not pass you by in quest of some rare and perfect tomorrow. Let me hold you while I may, for it will not always be so. One day I shall dig my nails into the earth, or bury my face in the pillow, or stretch myself taut, or raise my hands to the sky, and want, more than all the world, your return."

- Mary Jean Irion,
American writer and educator

Justin age 6

"When I was five years old, my mother told me that happiness was the key to life. When I went to school, my teacher asked what I wanted to be when I grew up. I wrote down "happy". She told me that I didn't understand the assignment, and I told my teacher that maybe she didn't understand life."

-John Lennon,
Singer/songwriter

CHAPTER 5

Early Childhood
Signs and Symptoms of Dyslexia

Genetics play important roles in determining one's human makeup. We all carry certain strengths and weaknesses that make us unique. Children born with dyslexia share this uniqueness, just like non-dyslexics. The difference lies in learning-style preference. Learning-style preferences are in our DNA and cannot be changed.

Learning-style preferences in humans have been part of our genetic pool for thousands of years. Our ancestors taught using kinesthetic approaches to learning, as reading from books did not exist. Over time however, teaching and learning by doing began disappearing, replaced by written words on a page.

An emphasis on learning by reading, along with one-way teaching, dominates our educational system. However, the dyslexic's learning style requires more emphasis on different teaching methods in order for them to learn, and which is why 30% of the world's population is not being taught the way they need to learn.

Although some schools have made efforts to recognize different learning styles among school-aged children, it is a laboriously slow acknowledgement. Knowing this, parents must educate themselves on the signs and symptoms of dyslexia to advocate and get help for their child.

The first five years of a child's life are most critical in the development stages of their emotional and physical health. When identifying signs of dyslexia, professional evaluators are looking for symptoms that are consistent with the disability. Parents can use the following guidelines, which may show a need for a formal evaluation:

- Dyslexia is in the family genes. If there are family members with dyslexia, the odds are high that offspring may inherit the gene. Family members who have similar symptoms but have not been assessed could also have dyslexia.

- Prone to ear infections. Newborns and toddlers may tug on their ears, cry and not want to eat. These are signs of an ear infection, which requires medical attention. Chronic ear infections can reoccur every two to three months, thereby interfering with sound, hearing and decoding of language. Children with recurring ear infections should be referred by their pediatrician to an otolaryngologist (ear, nose and throat physician specialist).

- Late crawling or walking. The dyslexic child may show less interest in wanting to crawl or walk until much later.

- Difficulty learning to tie shoelaces. This task has several steps and requires a specific order to be followed. This can be very challenging for dyslexic children because they cannot remember the order of the steps.

- Difficulty fastening buttons and/or getting dressed. These tasks can be confusing, daunting and frustrating to a child with dyslexia.

- Being ambidextrous (or late establishing a dominant hand). A dyslexic child may switch from one hand to the other during a single task, such as coloring, painting or drawing. Even after establishing a dominant hand, the dyslexic child may use one hand for writing and the other hand for sports.

- Delayed speech. Does not begin speaking words until two years of age or later, mispronounces words and/or still talks "baby talk."

- Mixing pronunciation sounds of multi-syllable words. Examples: saying aminal for animal, bisghetti for spaghetti, hekalopter for helicopter, or mazageen for magazine.

- Confusion with directional words and concepts. For example, right versus left, over versus under, and before versus after.

- Difficulty remembering/memorizing the names of letters or sounds in the alphabet. May also have difficulty reciting the alphabet in order or with words that rhyme.

- Difficulty memorizing. Young dyslexic children have difficulty learning and remembering their home address, telephone number or even date of birth. Their brain's short-term working memory is the issue.

- Bed wetting. Transitioning from diapers to underwear usually occurs between ages two and four. Dyslexic children may be trained during the day but will continue to wet their bed at night when sleeping. To overcome this, the brain needs to be trained to wake up when needing to go to the bathroom. We have more information regarding this subject on our website. (www.achildstouchstone.com)

- Extra deep sleeper. The brain is excessively tired because daily mental challenges require more effort. Extra deep sleep may also be part of the reason for bed wetting.

- Irritated or anxious in noisy environments or with competing sounds, when required to focus or listen (such as in a classroom environment).

- Difficulty following more than one instruction at a time. Children with dyslexia are often accused of "not listening" or "not paying attention."

- Difficulty recognizing rhyming patterns, such as cat, bat, rat and/or learning nursery rhymes.

- Difficulty expressing ideas or thoughts while involved in conversation, or unable to recall the right word, often pausing and using "um" or "like" to fill in the blanks.

- Difficulty remembering/memorizing numbers, days of the week, colors and/or shapes. Children with dyslexia often confuse days of the week with months of the year and vice versa.

- Difficulty catching, kicking or throwing a ball, hopping/skipping and/or clapping hands to a simple rhythm. Children with dyslexia are often falsely thought to be naturally uncoordinated or lacking in music ability.

- Difficulty understanding humor, puns or jokes. Grasping the punchline can be challenging because children with dyslexia require more time to process what is said.

- Clumsiness, dropping, spilling and/or knocking things over.

- Confusion between similar looking letters and/or numbers. Often thought to be letter and number reversals. Children with dyslexia do not see or read letters backwards.

- May not detect or respond properly to teasing. Children with dyslexia require more time to process information and therefore cannot quickly detect inappropriate behavior by others.

- Difficulty picking up on people's moods or feelings. Children with dyslexia often misinterpret what is said or observed and may say the wrong thing at the wrong time.

Knowing the early childhood symptoms of dyslexia, parents can act more quickly in discussing concerns with their child's pediatrician, who can then refer the child for evaluation with a clinical psychologist or pediatric neurologist who specializes in educational learning disabilities. These important first steps are necessary not only for a diagnosis but also to remove other possible concerns.

Parents should not delay having their child evaluated. Early detection is extremely important. The earlier the evaluation and diagnosis, the earlier interventions and therapies can begin and help their child.

Trevor age 7

"Why fit in, when you
were born to stand out?"

-Dr. Seuss
Author of children's books

CHAPTER 6

First and Second Grade
Signs and Symptoms of Dyslexia

Many signs and symptoms of dyslexia in a child become apparent in first and second grade. And teachers who have specific knowledge and training on dyslexia are more likely to refer for evaluation any child showing symptoms.

Below are typical symptoms of dyslexia for this age group and grade level. It is important to first read the previous chapter on early childhood signs and symptoms before reading this chapter. If a child has symptoms of dyslexia in first or second grade, they most likely showed signs in early childhood (during the first five years of life) that went unnoticed.

Parents and teachers seem surprised to learn many of the signs in early childhood are still present in grades one and two. That's because many of the symptoms of dyslexia accumulate and move forward in the child's life.

Signs and symptoms of dyslexia in first and second grade include the following:

- Often loses place while reading. Most reading materials, such as novels and textbooks, are not "reader friendly" for children with dyslexia. The type of font, text size, spacing between each word and the line spacing are often are too small, overcrowded and difficult for the dyslexic child to process properly.

- Lacks fluency while reading, often pausing mid-sentence. The brain is having to work twice as hard to process what is being read, which is why reading is slow and choppy.

- Recognizes a word in one sentence but not in the next. Parent(s) and teachers can often become easily frustrated with a child who cannot remember a word that they just read correctly a few sentences prior. It isn't the dyslexic child's fault. Their brain is trying to process many words in a sentence or paragraph and may not be able to remember everything that was just read.

- Often repeats reading mistakes over and over. Misinformed parents and teachers often assume that children with dyslexia should be able to self-correct and not repeat the mistake again. Children with dyslexia often repeat the same mistake over and over again because they are not being taught to their learning style.

- Difficulty "getting to the point." Although the dyslexic child may know inside what to say, quite often the words take a while to get out.

- Struggles with uneven printing, spacing between letters and words, and staying on the line. It is a common misconception that poor handwriting is due to weak finger dexterity when in fact it may be due to dyslexia.

- Confuses similar looking words, letters and/or numbers, such as pat/tap, b/d, and 6/9.

- Trouble telling time. The process of learning time with an analog clock requires many steps and can be mentally tiring to a child with dyslexia.

- Frequently mispronounces words. Dyslexic children often read phonetically because they lack the ability to properly sound out each consonant and vowel.

- Guesses or substitutes words while reading. A child with dyslexia who is unable to sound out a word will often compensate by guessing or substituting in another word to fill in the blank.

- Difficulty copying/writing, off the school board. The process of looking up at the board and down on the page, several times, is mentally exhausting to the dyslexic child. They often lose their place, rewrite already written work, or do not complete it within the required time.

- Difficulty working independently. Sometimes children with dyslexia are not given the appropriate attention during learning time and instead are required to work alone, with little or no assistance.

- Does not enjoy reading for pleasure. Most children naturally gravitate to visual story books and enjoy experiencing and learning new words associated with the story. If a child shows no interest or loses interest in reading for pleasure, something is wrong. This is a big "red flag" for parents and teachers.

- Often loses things. A dyslexic's short-term working memory is compromised, which is why they often forget where they have placed items.

- Has difficulty retelling what was just said or read. This is another area where parents and teachers become easily frustrated with a dyslexic child's inability to remember and retell a story or instructions. Short-term working memory issues are part of the reason.

- Inconsistent spelling (whether correct or not). Some teachers seem determined to fix a student's spelling issues by "red marking" or "marking off" for misspelled words, believing it will motivate the student to apply themselves. This strategy is futile.

- Difficulty learning/memorizing basic addition and subtraction facts. Depending on how the information is presented, children with dyslexia can become confused as to the meaning of addition and subtraction, similar to confusion over directions or left from right.

- Difficulty remembering new vocabulary words. If new vocabulary words are not presented kinesthetically, using all the senses to describe the word, the dyslexic student will most likely not retain the meaning or name of the word.

- Struggles with comprehension of ideas and themes. This is due to deficits in short-term working memory. Children with dyslexia do not lack comprehension. They lack the ability to remember what's learned long enough to transfer it into long-term memory. Teachers often suggest that certain children lack comprehension, when it is their short-term working memory that is the underlying problem.

- Forgetful in daily and routine activities. Children with dyslexia require clearly posted outlines of daily activities, especially those related to schoolwork, home responsibilities and extra curricular activities. They cannot remember numerous steps or activities by memory alone.

Life is an opportunity, benefit from it.

Life is beauty, admire it.

Life is bliss, taste it.

Life is a dream, realize it.

Life is a challenge, meet it.

Life is a duty, complete it.

Life is a game, play it.

Life is a promise, fulfill it.

Life is sorrow, overcome it.

Life is a song, sing it.

Life is a struggle, accept it.

Life is a tragedy, confront it.

Life is an adventure, dare it.

Life is luck, make it.

Life is too precious, do not destroy it.

Life is life, fight for it.

-Mother Teresa

Andrew age 11

"It's kind of fun doing the impossible."

-Walt Disney

CHAPTER 7

Third and Fourth Grade
Signs and Symptoms of Dyslexia

In third and fourth grade, students move from learning to read, to reading to learn. For children with dyslexia, struggling with reading, this transition is problematic. And without educational support and accommodations, most dyslexic students cannot academically keep up; they lag behind and are labeled as slow learners.

Below are typical symptoms of dyslexia for this age group and grade level. It's recommended to first read the two previous chapters on signs and symptoms of dyslexia for early childhood through second grade. If a child has symptoms of dyslexia in third and fourth grade, they most likely showed signs in early childhood, as well as in first and second grade, that went unnoticed. This is important because many symptoms of dyslexia accumulate and move forward in the child's life.

Signs and symptoms of dyslexia in third and fourth grade students (as well as in early childhood through second grade) include the following:

- Difficulty organizing homework assignments and due dates.

- Difficulty with "less than" and "greater than" comparisons.

- Difficulty joining in peer group conversation.

- Fears having to read aloud in class.

- Difficulty learning multiplication table.

- Difficulty sequencing thoughts when discussing or writing a story or essay.

- Difficulty with long division.

- Struggles with instructions that explain the concept of an assignment.

- Difficulty with mathematical word problems and needing visuals to complete the task.

- Inability to remember/memorize oral multiple instructions.

- Messy and incomplete writing/printing.

- Substitution or omission of words entirely when writing.

- Insertion of invented words into conversation.

- Difficulty proofing and self correcting schoolwork.

- Difficulty organizing home responsibilities, tasks and activities.

- Avoidance of reading aloud in class. (Is quiet and hoping to be invisible).

- Difficulty using correct punctuation and capitalization in written sentences.

- Misuse of words in conversation.

- Avoidance of reading, saying they're tired.

- Graded homework does not return home.

- Homework and assignments do not get turned into teacher.

- Homework to be completed goes missing.

- Use of both printing and cursive in the same word or sentence.

- Difficulty staying on task/topic during teacher instruction.

- Limited interest in novel-type books.

- Prevalence of difficulty with spelling and vocabulary.

- Difficulty responding or answering vague test questions.

- Struggles with math number alignment, which results in computation errors.

- Difficulty understanding concepts of time, money, measurements and fractions.

- Experiences being bullied by peers, including teasing, laughing and name calling.

- Begins throwing away poorly graded assignments and tests before they reach home.

- Begins to shy away from any attention in the classroom; does not want to be called upon by the teacher.

- Begins lying about homework turned in—that it was lost or someone took it.

- May not want to go to school.

- Doesn't want to complete daily homework; says it's too hard.

- Parent/teacher meetings show a drop in academic progress and lower grades.

- Remedial reading and phonics based programs do not improve the student's comprehension (short term and working memory).

Ben age 12

"Every student can learn, just not on the same day, or in the same way."

-George Evans,

Cartoonist/illustrator for comic books

CHAPTER 8

Fifth and Sixth Grade
Signs and Symptoms of Dyslexia

Children struggling academically in fifth and sixth grade need immediate attention. These students most likely have not been evaluated for a learning disability and are suffering academic failure. Their self-esteem is probably negatively affected and showing possible signs of sadness, depression, anger and not wanting to go to school.

The signs and symptoms of dyslexia begin in early childhood. It's therefore important to first read the three previous chapters on signs and symptoms of dyslexia for early childhood through fourth grade. If children have symptoms of dyslexia in fifth and sixth grade, they most likely showed symptoms of dyslexia in their younger years that went unnoticed. Many symptoms of dyslexia accumulate and move forward into the child's later years.

Signs and symptoms of dyslexia in fifth and sixth grade students (as well as in early childhood through fourth grade) include the following:

- Uses vague, imprecise language and has a limited vocabulary.

- Difficulty dealing with peer-group pressure, embarrassment and unexpected challenges.

- Difficulty taking notes and listening to teacher instructions at the same time.

- Uses poor grammar or misuses words during conversation.

- Avoids or is reluctant to engage in tasks that require sustained mental effort, such as homework.

- Performs inconsistently on tasks from one day to the next.

- Does not enjoy reading.

- Has a poor sense of direction.

- Is disorganized and poor at planning for future tests or assignments.

- Lacks basic writing skills equivalent to grade level. Has difficulty handwriting answers in sentences, paragraphs or essays.

- Cannot accurately copy notes from the classroom board.

- Cannot remember names of people, places, things and dates.

- Difficulty completing timed tests.

- Difficulty with word math problems. Unable to memorize order of mathematical operations.

- Difficulty understanding percentages and decimal conversions.

- Difficulty managing multiple tasks at the same time, especially if instructions are being presented in multiple ways, also at the same time.

- Difficulty understanding flat, two-dimensional drawings with three-dimensional views of actual objects.

- Difficulty summarizing main ideas and supporting details of a story.

- Difficulty applying skills from one situation to another.

- Is accused by parents and/or teachers of being lazy and/or unmotivated.

- Difficulty managing or is falling behind on core subject class assignments and/or homework.

- Feels overwhelmed; unable to complete tasks on time.

- Receives poor grades on tests.

- Lies about homework to be completed.

- Becomes uninterested in attending school.

- Seems disengaged and quiet while in class.

- Experiences continued peer bullying.

- Overall grades are slipping.

Lucy age 13

"Children often close their ears to advice,
but open their eyes to example."

-Anonymous

Seventh and Eighth Grade
Signs and Symptoms of Dyslexia

In seventh and eighth grade, students have increased academic demands from more than one teacher. Dyslexic students who have not been evaluated for a learning disability and are not receiving educational therapies or accommodations are at a tremendous disadvantage.

To fully understand all the signs and symptoms of dyslexia in children in seventh and eighth grade, it is important to first read the four previous chapters on signs and symptoms of dyslexia for early childhood through sixth grade. Children who have symptoms of dyslexia in seventh and eighth grade most likely showed symptoms of dyslexia in their younger years that went unnoticed. Many symptoms of dyslexia accumulate and move forward into the child's later years.

Signs and symptoms of dyslexia in seventh and eighth grade students (as well as early childhood through sixth grade), include the following:

- **Poor study skills and time management.** Good study habits involve organizing the content, as well as learning the disciplines necessary to complete the task. Successful study disciplines include a study buddy, which is usually left up to the student to organize. For children with dyslexia, the process is daunting, requiring several steps, with no guarantee of having someone to study with. Bottom line: Dyslexic students do not do well studying on their own.

- Difficulty learning a second (foreign) language. Dyslexic students find it very difficult to learn a second language. This is because their brain takes twice as long to process and/or decode information. However, an option for learning a second language is sign language. More and more high schools/colleges offer and accept sign language as meeting the second-language requirement.

- Poor note taking and outlining strategies. For dyslexic students, note taking (from the board or teacher) is never easy. The process of looking and up and down from the board and listening to the teacher at the same time is exhausting. And since the dyslexic student has not yet been evaluated for a learning disability, note taking and outlining of strategies has only gotten worse over the years.

- Difficulty discriminating between words with multiple meanings. Children with dyslexia have a difficult time discriminating similar looking words, as well as words with multiple meanings. This is because the brain takes longer to process and decode when reading.

- Oral language problems. Dyslexic students sometimes have difficulties communicating or understanding what they hear. They may not understand rhetorical questions, or they may misread a simple pun or joke.

- Poor reading comprehension. Children who struggle with comprehension are really struggling with short-term, working memory differences. Dyslexic students at this grade level will continue to struggle with poor reading comprehension unless knowledge is taught in ways that they can learn.

- Uninterested in reading. If not remediated, dyslexic students begin losing interest in reading early in their school years. By seventh and eighth grade, reading becomes a chore and is not enjoyed.

- Difficulties with mathematics. Some dyslexic students do well in math until word type problems, algebraic orders of operations and multiple step functions are introduced. Their short-term working memory has a difficult time processing and remembering all the necessary steps to complete the problem.

- Bullying by peers and others continues. Children with learning disabilities are often bullied by their peers, family members and teachers.

- Written work is incomplete or too brief. Students who have difficulty expressing written ideas often write brief essays rather than longer ones. Dyslexic students often struggle with written work because they're worried about their spelling, grammar, content and storyline, as well as how the teacher will grade everything. Sometimes it's just better to keep it short.

- Prefers to print, rather than write in cursive. Most dyslexic students at this grade level prefer to print if they believe their cursive writing is not legible enough to their teachers. Some teachers, beginning as early as first grade, criticize student handwriting as sloppy or illegible. Over time, this type of criticism takes its toll on dyslexic students, and they begin denying their own abilities to learn cursive and/or write properly.

- Poor short-term working memory. Children with dyslexia do not outgrow short-term working memory weaknesses. Academic support is what helps improve their ability to learn.

- Failing grades. If dyslexic students have not been evaluated and identified with a learning disability, their grades are going to show less-than-positive results.

- Frustration by teachers and parents. The dyslexic student continues to fall behind academically. Teachers and parents are often frustrated, even angry, because the student seems disengaged due to the inability to learn.

Zac age 17

"Teenagers are the most misunderstood
people on Earth. We are treated like
children but expected to act like adults."

-Anonymous

CHAPTER 10

Ninth through Twelfth Grade Signs and Symptoms of Dyslexia

High school students with undiagnosed learning disabilities suffer tremendous academic failure. Their struggles in school are much worse, and parents and teachers may point fingers, blaming each other for the student's academic failure.

In most cases, undiagnosed dyslexic high school students are barely passing their courses, in jeopardy of being retained, and not on track for twelfth-grade completion. Homework is often an upsetting experience—crying, not knowing how to complete math problems, frustration at having to read 50 pages, not remembering most of it and hurting because of the constant negative feedback.

As described in the first five chapters on the signs and symptoms of dyslexia for early childhood through eighth grade, dyslexia symptoms are cumulative and present themselves throughout a child's formidable years. It is important to first read these five chapters, if you have not already done so, before reading this one.

Signs and symptoms of dyslexia in ninth through twelfth grade students (as well as early childhood through eighth grade), include the following:

- Teacher(s) indicate the student is:

  - Lazy and/or unmotivated.

  - Not working up to his/her potential.

  - Not trying hard enough—could do better if more effort was made.

- Not paying attention during teacher instruction.

- Unable to complete in-classroom work on time.

- Slow at copying from the board.

- Apparently unable to understand what the teacher wants.

- Unable to produce good handwriting and spell correctly.

- Slow to respond when called upon.

- Struggles with completing homework. Dyslexic students often cannot understand the homework, nor do they have enough time to complete it accurately before the due date.

- Difficulty remembering multiple-step directions. For example, a dyslexic child would have a hard time following through completely if told, "We're going out for dinner. Go wash your face and hands, put on your blue shirt and beige pants and don't forget to brush your hair."

- Experiences tremendous stress and fatigue during test finals. Tests are not easily accessible. Multiple choice questions are laced with double negatives, essay questions are vague, font and text size are inappropriate, test pages are overcrowded and instructions require flipping back and forth from question to answer.

- Difficulty with oral presentations. The load on memory, organizational problems, reading aloud from notes and the added stress from past experiences are enough to deter most dyslexic students from presenting thoughts in front of their classmates and teacher. Has difficulty contributing to small and large group discussions.

- Other areas of concern include:

  - Substantial difficulties mastering mathematical facts.

  - Limited vocabulary and communication with peers and adults.

- Lack of confidence and self esteem.

- Slow reading speed, well below grade level.

- Extremely poor written expression; large discrepancy between verbal and written communication.

- Anxiety and frustration. Easily overwhelmed by multiple tasks.

- Perception of self as a poor learner.

- Feeling unprepared during academic testing.

- Lack of enjoyment of reading, finding it grueling and exhausting.

- Hesitation in taking risks involving individual projects, choosing instead simple, less challenging topics or tasks.

- Poor ability for navigation and sense of direction.

- Low expectations by teacher(s) of student ability.

- Being bullied.

- Inability to finish tests on time, or else rushing and making careless errors, which do not reflect their knowledge on the subject.

- Inability to master a foreign language.

- Weak problem solving/coping skills.

- Possible depression or feelings of sadness.

- Difficulty making and keeping friends. Poor social judgment.

- Poor grades in most class subjects.

- Desire to quit school.

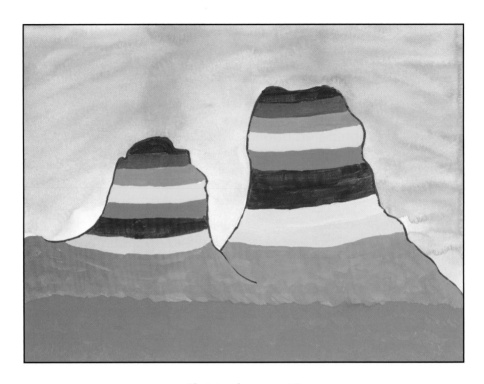

Christopher age 10

"Everything you can imagine is real."

-Pablo Picasso, Artist

CHAPTER 11

The Right-Brain Dyslexic

It's a fact that humans use both sides of their brain every day. Both the right and left sides of the brain have specific responsibilities and work together in performing a wide variety of tasks. Differences in right- and left-brain dominance occur when the responsibilities in different areas of the brain indicate stronger abilities above the norm. An exaggerated example would be an illiterate person with great artistic ability.

Most dyslexics are right-brain dominant. They process information conceptually and pictorially, rather than orally and sounding out of words. The following helps to explain how dyslexics process information:

- Visual processing is a strength, not a weakness. Dyslexics process more effectively in pictures, drawings and shapes. Dyslexics usually remember visual details, see differences between things, enjoy art and exhibit strengths in visualization and imagination. In some respects, dyslexics can see in 3 D. When looking at an object, they can view it simultaneously from different perspectives. This is good for creativity, but not so good for reading.

- When a visual image is over-crowded or cluttered with too much visual information (including text, symbols, pictures, etc.), the dyslexic's visual processing suffers. Over-crowded visual information can negatively affect areas of math, spelling and writing, reading speed, comprehension, work accuracy and organization.

- Right brain processing involves looking for "the big picture," which is why most dyslexics are highly creative and inventive. They "see" things first and then describe them, which is why dominant left-brain teaching (areas associated with phonetic decoding) are ineffective when taught exclusively using right-brain activities. Without a focus on teaching conceptual understanding, instruction becomes memorization of meaningless facts and procedures.

- The right side of the brain does most of the thinking, reasoning and creating. It has lots of wonderful ideas, but it cannot properly organize them fast enough for expression, such as in writing. The dyslexic's right-brain is working fast, but it's the left side of the brain that is responsible for organizing these thoughts and ideas (in short-term working memory). In contrast, a left-brained person is usually very good at memorizing and organizing, but slower in generating new ideas or understanding concepts.

- Right-brain conceptual processing with dyslexics includes strengths in rhythm and music, but difficulty in reading comprehension, math reasoning and creative writing, which are weaknesses in slower processing speed.

- Visual processing enters information into the brain first; this is a dyslexic's strength. Sequential processing (memory) to remember, finishes the task; this is a dyslexic's weakness.

- Kinesthetic and visual instruction and learning work best. Verbal instruction is least effective. ("I can hear you, I just can't understand you.") Kinesthetic instruction involves hands on learning, such as building a 3-dimensional object for a mathematical assignment. Visual instruction involves drawings, pictures, movement and imagination. Visual learners see pictures of what the word is and not the symbols of the word as written.

- Dyslexics use forms of thought in which images recalled in the brain can then be rotated, increased or decreased in size, overlaid or otherwise transformed from one familiar image into another, similar to what takes place during digital imaging processing. Layers of images overlay each other to form the completed result.

- Dyslexics need to visualize the desired result described by the teacher, understand what is visually occurring during the steps or process, and why the answer or result is correct. If these steps are not included during the learning process, dyslexics will become disengaged as a result of boredom.

- Dyslexics need questions and assignments around a given conclusion or fact, (as previously described). Dyslexic students think in concrete wholes, that is, they work backwards from a conclusion or fact, to fill in all the parts. This process is also known as "top/down processing."

- Dyslexic children do not process "open ended" questions, such as "Which lines are parallel?" when it is just as easy to ask, "Which lines are parallel to each other?" Visualize four lines, two of which are facing two different directions.

- Dyslexics need to read the beginning, then the end, and then the middle of a chapter story. Presenting the end of the story after the beginning gives the dyslexic "the big picture" and thereby increases their comprehension. It's like playing a sport, such as hockey, before learning the formal plays and strategy of the game. There is prior attained ability and insight into the game, which makes it easier to understand the concept and result. Any prior knowledge, whether it be through watching a movie or acting out a play, is extremely beneficial to the learning process.

- Dyslexics need encouragement when using their natural right-brain traits and talents, including artistic abilities in different mediums, athletic talents, creative imaginations and out-of-the-box thinking and problem-solving skills.

- Dyslexics prefer to see, feel, touch, taste, smell and hear things. They prefer to experience life in the present. If there is a history lesson on World War II, dyslexic students prefer to close their eyes and listen to President Franklin Roosevelt's declaration-of-war radio message, while visualizing the President's deep concern or anticipation in doing so.

- Right-brain dominant dyslexics think emotionally, intuitively and creatively, and they want to know the big picture.

"You're alive. Do Something. The directive in life, the moral imperative was so uncomplicated. It could be expressed in single words, not complete sentences. It sounded like this: Look. Listen. Choose. Act."

-Barbara Hall,
Canadian lawyer, 61st Mayor
of Toronto, Canada

Ethan age 11

"If you are lucky enough to
be different, don't change."

-Anonymous

CHAPTER 12

Learning-Style Preference

It would be a very boring world if we all thought and learned the same way. Thank goodness each of us has our own natural learning style preference that is as unique as our fingerprints.

Each of us processes information depending on our brain (left or right side) dominance, our preferred thinking style. It makes sense then, that children take in and process learning of new information in different ways.

Students can benefit from understanding their own learning style preferences and applying these tools to academic learning. If teachers understand their students' learning style preferences, they can apply differentiated teaching methods that will benefit academic learning. The key is to match the teaching style of instruction with student learning style in order to achieve a positive balance. When this method is successfully applied, students and teachers are more in sync with each other and a new rhythm of learning takes place.

The next few pages contain a learning-style preference questionnaire that can be used to determine a student's learning style.

Note: All forms, in 8 ½" x 11" (letter size), are available with ownership (purchase) of A Child's Touchstone. Go to www.achildstouchstone.com to download them for your use.

Learning-Style Preference

STUDENT NAME: _____

STUDENT I.D. # _____

DATE OF BIRTH: _____ GRADE: _____ GENDER: _____

SCHOOL: _____

This questionnaire has been designed to help identify ways in which a student learns best in an academic/school environment.

Read each statement and check the box, using the following rating system, which best describes your preference:

4 = ALMOST ALWAYS **3** = FREQUENTLY **2** = SOMETIMES **1** = HARDLY EVER

		4	3	2	1
1	When I "make things" for my schoolwork, I remember what I learned better.				
2	Written assignments are easy for me.				
3	I learn better if someone reads to me, than when I read silently to myself.				
4	I learn more when I study with a group of students.				
5	Having assignment directions written on the board makes them easier to understand.				
6	It's harder for me to do a written assignment than an oral one.				

(Continued on the next page)

		4	3	2	1
7	When I do math problems in my head, I say the numbers to myself.				
8	If I need help on a subject, I will ask a classmate.				
9	I understand a math problem that is written down, better than one I hear.				
10	I don't mind doing written assignments.				
11	I remember things I hear, better than I read.				
12	I remember more of what I learn, if I learn it when I am alone.				
13	I would rather read a story than listen to it read.				
14	I feel like I "talk" smarter than I write.				
15	If someone tells me 3 numbers to add, I can usually get the right answer without writing them down.				
16	I prefer to work in a group because I learn from the others.				
17	Written math problems are easier for me to do than oral ones.				
18	Writing a spelling word several times helps me remember it better.				
19	I find it easier to remember what I have heard than what I have read.				
20	It is more fun to learn with classmates at first, but it is hard to study with them.				
21	I like written directions better than spoken ones.				

(Continued on the next page)

		4	3	2	1
22	If homework were oral, I would do it all.				
23	When I hear a phone number, I can remember it without writing it down.				
24	I get more work done when I work with someone.				
25	Seeing a number makes more sense to me than hearing a number.				
26	I like to do things, like simple repairs or crafts with my hands.				
27	The things I write on paper sound better than when I say them.				
28	I study best when no one is around to talk or listen to.				
29	I would rather read things in a book than have the teacher tell me about them.				
30	Speaking is a better way than writing, if I want someone to understand it better.				
31	When I have a written math problem to do, I say it to myself to understand it better				
32	I can learn more about a subject if I am with a small group of students.				
33	Seeing the price of something written down is easier for me to understand than having someone tell me the price.				
34	I like to make things with my hands.				
35	I like tests that call for sentence completion or written answers.				
36	I understand more from a class discussion than from reading about a subject.				

(Continued on the next page)

		4	3	2	1
37	I remember the spelling of a word better if I see it written down than if someone spells it aloud.				
38	Spelling and grammar rules make it hard for me to say what I want when writing it.				
39	It makes it easier when I say the numbers of a problem to myself as I work it out.				
40	I like to study with other people.				
41	When a teacher says a number, I really don't understand it until I see it written down.				
42	I understand what I have learned, better when I am involved in making something for the subject.				
43	Sometimes I say silly things, but writing gives me time to correct myself.				
44	I do well on tests if they are about things I hear in class.				
45	I can't think as well when I work with someone as when I work alone.				

Scoring: Visual Language (VL)

Question	Score
5	
13	
21	
29	
37	
Total	
Score = Total x 2	

Scoring: Visual-Numerical (VN)

Question	Score
9	
17	
25	
33	
41	
Total	
Score – Total x 2	

Scoring: Auditory-Language (AL)

Question	Score
3	
11	
19	
36	
44	
Total	
Score = Total x 2	

Scoring: Auditory-Numerical (AN)

Question	Score
7	
15	
23	
31	
39	
Total	
Score = Total x 2	

Scoring: Auditory-Visual-Kinesthetic (AVK)

Question	Score
1	
18	
26	
34	
42	
Total	
Score = Total x 2	

Scoring: Social-Individual (SI)

Question	Score
4	
12	
20	
28	
45	
Total	
Score = Total x 2	

Scoring: Social-Group (SG)

Question	Score
8	
16	
24	
32	
40	
Total	
Score = Total x 2	

Scoring: Expressive-Oral (EO)

Question	Score
6	
14	
22	
30	
38	
Total	
Score = Total x 2	

Scoring: Expressive-Written (EW)

Question	Score
2	
10	
27	
35	
43	
Total	
Score = Total x 2	

		VL	VN	AL	AN	AVK
Major Learning Style Preference	34-40					
Minor Learning Style Preference	20-32					
Negligible	10-18					

		SI	SG	EO	EW
Major Learning Style Preference	34-40				
Minor Learning Style Preference	20-32				
Negligible	10-18				

See next page for explanation of learning styles.

Definitions and Teaching Techniques for Major Learning Styles

The following are descriptions of learning styles found in every learner to a major, minor, or negligible extent and teaching suggestions related to each learning style.

Learning Style	Teaching Techniques
Visual-Learning (VL): This student learns well from seeing words in books, on the board, charts of workbooks. He or she may write words down that are given orally in order to learn by seeing them on paper. They remember and use information better if it has been read first.	Student will benefit from a variety of books and written materials on several levels of difficulty. Given time alone with a book, he or she may learn more than during class. Make sure important information is provided in written form or through note taking, in order for the student to remember specific details.

Learning Style	Teaching Techniques
Visual-Numerical (VN): This student must see the numbers on the board, in a book, or on paper, in order to learn effectively. They're more likely to remember and understand math facts that are presented visually, than with oral presentation.	Student will benefit from worksheets, workbooks and texts. Provide a variety of written materials and allow time to study it. Math games and activities are best played in written format. All important data should be given on paper.

Learning Style	Teaching Techniques
Auditory-Language (AL): This student learns best from hearing spoken words. When striving to understand and remember material, they often speak softly or move their lips while reading.	Student will benefit from listening to audio recordings, rote oral practice, lectures or class discussion. He or she may benefit from recording instructions to listen to later, by teaching/tutoring another student, or conversing with the teacher. Groups of two or more, games or interaction activities, provide the sounds of words being spoken that are so important to this student.

Learning Style	Teaching Techniques
Auditory-Numerical (AN): This student learns best from hearing numbers and oral explanations. He or she may remember telephone and locker numbers with ease, and be successful with oral numbers, games and puzzles. They do just as well without a math book, because written materials are not as important to them. This student can work out most math problems in their head. You may hear the student saying the numbers aloud or see their lips moves, as a problem is read.	Student will benefit from math with audio recordings or from working with other people while talking about a problem. Reading written explanations aloud will also help. Games or activities in which number problems are spoken, will help. Student will benefit from tutoring others or delivering an explanation to his or her study group, or teacher.

Learning Style	Teaching Techniques
Auditory-Visual-Kinesthetic (AVK): This student learns best be experience and self-involvement. He or she definitely needs a combination of stimuli. The manipulation of material, along with the accompanying sights and sounds (words and numbers seen and spoken) make a big difference. The student may not seem able to understand, or keep his or her mind on work unless totally involved in the process, including handling, touching and working with what is being learned. Hand-doodle writing or a symbolic wriggling of the fingers, are signs of the AVK learner.	Student must be given more than just reading and math assignments. Involve him or her with at least one other student and provide an activity related to the assignment. Accompany an audio recording, with pictures, objects and an activity, such as drawing, writing and/or following directions with physical movement.

Learning Style	Teaching Techniques
Social-Individual (SI): This students gets more work done, thinks best and remembers more when alone. He or she cares more for their own opinions than the ideas of others. You will not have much trouble keeping this student from over-socializing during class.	Student needs to be allowed to do important learning alone. If you feel he or she needs socialization, save it for a non-learning situation. Let this student go to the library or work alone in the classroom. Sometimes, students who prefer to work alone become easily irritated by the distraction of group work. Some great thinkers are lone workers.

Learning Style	Teaching Techniques
Social-Group (SG): This student strives to study with at least one other student, as he or she will not get as much done working alone. They value others ideas and preferences. Group interaction increases their learning and later recognition of facts. Socializing is important to this student.	Student needs to do important with someone else. The stimulation of the group is more important in their learning process.

Learning Style	Teaching Techniques
Expressive-Oral (EO): This student prefers to tell what they know. He or she talks fluently, comfortable, and clearly. The teacher may find this learner knows more than written tests show. This student is typically less shy than others while giving oral reports, or talking to classmates or teachers. The muscular coordination involved in writing however, may be difficult for this learner. Organizing and putting thoughts on paper may be too slow and tedious a task for EO students.	Allow student to present oral reports instead of written ones. Whether in conference, small or large group, evaluate him or her more by what is said, than by what is written. Reports can be recorded to save class time. Do however, require a minimum amount of written work.

Learning Style	Teaching Techniques
Expressive-Written (EW): This student can write fluent essays, and good answers on tests to show what he or she knows. They're less comfortable when oral answers are required. Their thoughts are better organized on paper, than when given orally.	Student needs to be allowed to write reports, keep notebooks and journals for credit and take written tests for evaluation. Oral presentations should be under non-pressured conditions, perhaps even in a one-to-one conference.

Student Understanding:

<u>Visual</u> "Major" Learning Style Preference:

You learn well from "seeing words" in books, on the board and in textbooks. You remember and understand information and instructions better if you read them. You don't need as much oral explanation as an auditory learner, and you can often learn alone, with a book. You should take notes of lectures and oral directions if you want to remember the information.

Note: Visual learners often feel lost in a classroom where oral instruction and verbal discussion are the main teaching methods. Quite often they imagine a mental picture of what is being said, or visualize the words that are being spoken. Visual learners reproduce information best through demonstration by expressing themselves in writing or drawing.

<u>Auditory</u> "Major" Learning Style Preference:

You learn from "hearing words" spoken and from oral explanations. You remember information by reading aloud or moving your lips as you read, especially when you are learning new material. You benefit from hearing audio recordings, lectures, and class discussions. You benefit from making tapes/cd's to listen to, by teaching other students, and by conversing with your teacher.

Note: Auditory learners learn well in a classroom environment based around a lecture or discussion, but may find it difficult to learn information from a textbook or remember events in a story.

<u>Kinesthetic</u> "Major" Learning Style Preference:

You learn best by experience, by being involved physically in the classroom experiences. You remember information well when you actively participate in activities, field trips, and role-playing in the classroom. Kinesthetic learners will often fidget, pace the floor, tap a pencil or toss a ball up in the air and catch it.

Note: Kinesthetic learning style refers to doing, moving and acting, with characteristics that include:

- Being energetic and enjoyment of moving.

- Hands-on activities.

- Thinking and learning best when they are active.

Note: Some ways to appeal to kinesthetic learners include:

- Having students "do" rather than watch or listen.

- Incorporating activities that requirement movement, such as games, sports and dancing.

- Teaching content in terms of real-life situations.

- Role play various characters or act out scenes.

Tactile "Major" Learning Style Preference:

You learn best when you have the opportunity to do "hands on" experiences with materials. That is, working on experiments in a laboratory, handling and building models, and touching and working with materials provide you with the most successful learning situation. Writing notes or instructions can help you remember information, and physical involvement in class related activities may help you understand new information.

Group "Major" Learning Style Preference:

You learn more easily when you study with at least one other student, and you will be more successful completing work well when you work with others. You value group interaction and class work with other students, and you remember information better when you work with two or three classmates. The stimulation you receive from group work helps you learn and understand new information.

Individual "Major" Learning Style Preference:

You learn best when you work alone. You think better when you study alone, and you remember information you learn by yourself. You understand new material best when you learn it alone, and you make better progress in learning when you work by yourself.

Minor Learning Styles – In most cases, minor learning styles indicate areas where you can function well as a learner. Usually a very successful learner can learn in several different ways.

Negligible Learning Styles – Often, a negligible score indicates that you may have difficulty learning in that way. One solution may be to direct your learning to your stronger styles. Another solution might be to try to work on some of the skills to strengthen your learning style in the negligible area.

Carson age 10

"Be a voice, not an echo.
Stand up for what you believe in."

-Anonymous

CHAPTER 13

Listening

The ability to listen comes naturally to most people. Over time, we develop strong senses that help with listening and learning. For others, their listening ability is hampered by a sensory deficit (typically with sense of hearing).

As with dyslexia, a listening deficit cannot be seen. It is only through a formal evaluation measuring receptive and expressive listening ability that a listening deficit is known.

Research has found that people with dyslexia have more trouble recognizing voices, including problems with how their brain processes speech while putting together words from smaller units of sound. Knowing this, and that dyslexia is genetic and runs in families, parents should be alert to possible listening deficits in their children, which could be an early indicator of dyslexia.

It is important to understand what listening represents and what symptoms are typical of listening deficits.

Turn the page and learn the differences in listening ability.......

Receptive listening focuses "outside" of the self, no matter what others are saying, or what is going on in the work, school or home environment. Receptive listening deficits can include:

- Difficulty staying focused.

- Short attention span.

- Easily distracted by noise and overly sensitive to everyday sounds.

- Overly sensitive to certain sounds.

- Misinterpreting of questions or requests.

- Difficulty with sound discrimination.

- Confuses similar sounding words.

- Requires repeated clarification of instruction.

- Difficulty following one or two instructions in a sequence.

- Difficulty understanding group discussions.

- Poor short-term memory.

- Poor long-term memory.

- Must read material several times in an effort to absorb content.

- Tires easily.

- Becomes sleepy when listening to instructor speak or read aloud.

- Difficulty hearing low male voices.

- Difficulty hearing high female voices.

- Believes that most people speak too fast for their understanding.

- Difficulty listening in crowded places or while talking on the telephone.

- Difficulty differentiating between different tones and sounds.

- Needs more time to think of a response.

Expressive listening focuses "inside" the self, include checking, monitoring and reproducing correctly what one hears, especially one's own voice and speech. Expressive listening deficits include:

- Flat and monotonous voice quality.

- Lack of fluency in speech, and rhythm is hesitant.

- Difficulty recalling exact word usage.

- Weak vocabulary.

- Poor sentence structure.

- Overuse of stereotyped expressions.

- Singing out of tune.

- Difficulty with reading, especially aloud.

- Poor spelling.

- Difficulty summarizing a story.

- Difficulty relating isolated facts.

- Stumbling over words.

- Difficulty learning foreign languages.

Motor skills involve "listening to the body." These skills are related to the integration of several sensory systems and involve balance, coordination, body image, spatial awareness and temporal orientation. Motor skills deficits include:

- Poor posture, including slouching and slumping.

- Inadequate sense of personal space or physical boundaries.

- Atypical drive for movement and/or touch.

- Uncoordinated body movement.

- Fidgeting.

- Clumsiness, including tripping and stumbling.

- Confusion of right and left.

- Frequent confusion about location and direction.

- Poor sense of rhythm and/or timing of movement.

- Poor athletic skills.

- Messy handwriting.

- Difficulty with organization and structure.

- Ambidextrous sometimes, but not always.

A wide variety of behaviors and attitudes may be related to listening deficits, including:

- Low frustration tolerance—temper tantrums.

- Poor self-image or low self-confidence.

- Difficulty in making and keeping friends.

- Shyness—withdraws from or avoids social interactions.

- Inordinately tired at end of school day.

- Low motivation, minimal interest in school, little desire to participate.

- Tense and anxious.

- Limited sense of aliveness.

- Difficulty setting goals and priorities.

- Difficulty beginning and completing projects.

- Difficulty with time concepts and punctuality.

- Difficulty making judgments and generalizing to new situations.

- Hesitant to accept responsibility.

- Does not complete assignments.

- Lack of tactfulness.

- Tendency to act immaturely.

- Does not tolerate stress well.

- Bullied by students at school.

- Negative reports of frustration by teachers regarding student performance.

The ears act as a dynamo, providing us with electrical energy that affects the brain and nervous system. This energy is necessary for our survival and for us to achieve fulfilling lives. Problems with levels of energy may include:

- Difficulty getting up in the morning.

- Tiredness at the end of the day.

- Habit of procrastinating.

- Hyperactivity.

- Tendency toward depression.

- Feels overburdened with everyday tasks.

Listening difficulties usually develop early in life, from infancy through age five. It is during these first five years that we are also learning language by processing information to our brain through our ears, eyes and nose (hearing, seeing and smelling), as well as through touch and taste. Therefore, any interference that prevents normal development during these years can negatively impact a child's learning development—a critical stage in life.

Interferences in developing our senses can occur during a stressful pregnancy or difficult delivery, concussion or head trauma or exposure to excessive loud sounds. It can also be caused by recurring ear infections, which is true of 20 to 30% of the world population.

Research indicates that children who have recurring ear infections are 50% more likely to develop listening deficits.

Listening deficits can negatively impact or exacerbate the learning process for children with dyslexia. If dyslexic children perceive sounds differently in their right or left ear, then discrimination of sound can have a major impact on development of language and literacy.

Children with dyslexia who have frequent, recurring ear infections can experience such side effects as these:

- Mild to moderate fluctuating hearing loss, which means they receive partial or inconsistent auditory signals.

- Appearing to be distracted and disorganized.

- Disruption in auditory input, which affects phonological awareness and speech-processing skills.

- Incomplete and inaccurate encoding of information from which language develops.

- Frequent changes in the intensity of auditory signals and therefore learn to "tune out."

- Missing spoken instruction or requests.

- Distractibility.

- Difficulty working independently.

Deficits in a child's listening ability will, in all cases, affect listening comprehension. Listening comprehension involves the ability to understand, remember and discuss the meaning of words heard, and to retell it in their own words. Early detection of possible listening deficits in a child could be an early indicator of dyslexia.

Carmen age 8

"Very often the vision comes slowly, bit by bit, like a scene set on the stage. At other times, however, it is sudden and fleeting. Something passes before your eyes, and it must be seized quickly or it is lost".

-Gustave Flaubert, Poet

CHAPTER 14

Seeing a Learning Disability

Young children don't know the difference between good eyesight and not so good eyesight, which is why examinations, given at various ages from birth through eighteen, are so important. Parents rely on their child's pediatrician or family doctor to refer their child for further visual testing as needed, or when the child is showing signs of struggling in school, which could be signs of a learning disability. A referral is usually made to an optometrist, pediatric ophthalmologist or vision therapist.

The point of the referral is to determine if the child has a visual deficit, and if so, to initiate the appropriate remediation necessary to improve or correct the eye's weaknesses.

Some parents rely heavily on visual screenings that take place at school. Unfortunately, most school-provided visual screenings are not thorough enough or equipped to determine whether a child's brain is accurately processing what they are seeing. This is because most screenings only cover basic "distance" vision and maybe "near" vision, if you're lucky.

Relying exclusively on a child's school for visual screening is insufficient. A child's pediatrician or family doctor is more knowledgeable in determining visual deficits and is also able to write an immediate prescription for further evaluation. It's extremely important that parents be honest with the physician as to their child's academic school performance because it may be attributed to vision deficits.

All visual screenings should include an "Eye Teaming Test." This is because 75% of children with learning disabilities have poor visual skills. Extensive visual screenings by qualified professionals may identify early signs of a learning disability, such as dyslexia. The earlier the detection, the more support is available in helping children with dyslexia.

"You were born to be
real, not to be perfect."

- Anonymous

Brandon age 11

"To be in your child's memories
tomorrow, you have to be
in their lives today."

-Barbara Johnson
American Literary Critic

CHAPTER 15

Areas of Evaluation
for Diagnosing Dyslexia

As previously discussed in chapter 3, these eight areas affect learning:

- Listening comprehension

- Oral expression

- Written expression

- Basic reading skill

- Reading fluency

- Reading comprehension

- Math calculation

- Math reasoning/problem solving

If a child is suspected of having a specific learning disability, such as dyslexia, a professional evaluation should include:

- Listening comprehension (in language)—the ability to understand, remember and discuss the meaning of words heard, and to re tell it in their own words. Areas of concern:

  - Auditory short-term working memory

  - Long-term memory association

  - Auditory processing speed

  - Phonological processing (sounds given to language)

- Oral expression—the ability to verbally communicate ideas and thoughts. Areas of concern:

  - Motor coordination processing

  - Executive functions

- Basic reading skills—

  1. The ability to read text, such as being able to recognize and name letters of the alphabet, or commonly used words (sight word recognition). Areas of concern:

     - Short-term working memory

     - Long-term memory processing

  2. The ability to read and sound out words and their syllables, to recognize similar-sounding words and silent letters in words and to separate or mix sounds to form new words. Area of concern:

     - Phonemic awareness

  3. The ability to understand the relationships between written letters and spoken words (phonics) with the ability to visually identify letters and words (orthographic processing), and distinguish the differences in known and unknown words (word analysis skills). Area of concern:

     - Auditory or visual processing

  4. The ability to understand the meaning of word parts, such as prefixes, roots and suffixes.

- Reading fluency—the ability to read text with speed (at an appropriate rate), accuracy and proper expression (intonation). Areas of concern:

  - Processing speed

  - Auditory processing and auditory working memory

  - Associative memory

- Reading Comprehension—the ability to derive meaning from what is being read, and to demonstrate an understanding of its content. Areas of concern:

  - Fluid reasoning

  - Morphological awareness

  - Processing speed

  - Executive memory

  - Executive functions

  - Sustained attention and successive processing

- Written expression—the ability to communicate ideas, thoughts and feelings in written form, organized into words with correct syntax, grammar and spelling. Areas of concern:

  - Orthographic processing

  - Oral expression

  - Fluid reasoning

  - Working memory

  - Executive functions (planning and organizing)

  - Motor coordination

  - Phonological awareness

- Math calculation/computation—the ability to apply mathematical symbols and order of operations when solving math calculations and word problems. Areas of concern include:

  - Processing speed

  - Working memory

  - Long-term associative memory

- Math reasoning/problem solving—the ability to use decision making skills in math concepts and to apply them in real world situations. This includes comprehension of math problems and showing one's work. Areas of concern:

  - Fluid reasoning

Many tests are available for evaluating specific learning disabilities and symptoms of dyslexia. However, depending on the qualifications and education of the school psychologist, educational specialist or evaluator, some may use only one or two tests in determining a learning disability. They may find one or no weaknesses and assume there are no others. This is problematic, as they can come to a wrong or incomplete conclusion.

Parents, teachers and pediatricians need to be aware that not all evaluations are complete or correct and that further evaluation may be necessary. Below is a list of possible areas of identification that can affect a child's ability to learn:

- Auditory discrimination problem

- Auditory processing disorder

- Central auditory processing disorder

- Orthographic deficit

- Developmental reading disorder

- Dysnomia

- Dysphonetic deficit

- Phonemic awareness deficit

- Reading disability

- Reading fluency problem

- Short-term or long-term memory deficit

- Specific language disability

- Spelling patterns problem

- Visual processing disorder

- Visual motor integration disorder

- Visual memory deficit

- Visual tracking problem

- Visual convergence problem

- Vocabulary-on-demand problem

- Word retrieval deficit

- Written language disorder

Weakness in one area should always be followed up with additional testing in other areas, which can then lead to symptoms of dyslexia.

Max age 14

"My father use to say - Don't raise
your voice. Improve your argument."

-Archbishop Desmond Tutu
South African social rights activist

CHAPTER 16

Teacher Referral for Student Evaluation

When properly trained, teachers are first to notice when a student with appropriate teacher instruction is struggling academically. Such observations should immediately trigger an "action plan" that includes the following:

- Arrange a face-to-face meeting with the student's parent(s).

  Prior to the meeting, the teacher(s) should complete the Teacher Observations worksheets (included in this book), covering the areas of Listening Comprehension, Oral Expression, Basic Reading Skills, Reading Fluency, Reading Comprehension, Written Expression, Math Computation, Math Reasoning/Problem Solving and Student Productivity. These worksheets are designed for easy completion and understanding and will assist the teacher(s) and parent(s) while discussing the student's challenges and strengths. A copy of the completed Teacher Observations worksheets should be provided to the parents for this purpose and their records.

- Depending on the grade of the student, provide the parent(s) with the appropriate Parent Observation Worksheet(s) (also included in this book), for their completion during the meeting. Although these forms are designed for easy completion and understanding, teachers should have the same worksheets in front of them and offer assistance if needed. A copy of the completed Parent Observations worksheet(s) should be retained by the teacher(s).

- Upon completion of the Parent Observations worksheet(s), a discussion regarding items on the completed worksheet should immediately follow. Tremendous insight can be gleaned for both teacher and parent(s). This is an opportunity to learn about the student on a more personal level and for the teacher and parent(s) to interject similar childhood experiences. It is important to include concerns regarding stress, fear, anxiety or bullying that the student may be also experiencing. These concerns humanize the meeting.

- Share with the parent(s), student work samples, while explaining (as noted on the Teacher Observations worksheets) which area(s) of academic learning are showing weakness. This will help guide the parent(s) into better understanding teacher concerns. The teacher should refrain from suggesting that the student has great potential and just needs to work a little harder. (If properly trained, the teacher(s) will know better than to suggest this.)

- Be prepared to suggest referring the student for an evaluation for possible academic learning weaknesses in the area(s) of listening comprehension, oral expression, written expression, basic reading skill, reading fluency, reading comprehension, math calculation and/or math reasoning/problem solving, as indicated on the Teacher Observations worksheets. It is the teacher's responsibility to accurately communicate concerns and recommendations, based on their professional educational training, experience and overall knowledge of learning disabilities.

- Complete the Teacher Referral for Student Evaluation (included in this book) and provide a copy to the parent(s). Optionally, the parent(s) can also write a letter requesting that their child be referred for evaluation. (A sample letter is included in this book.)

- Provide the parent(s) with an Evaluation Process summary sheet (included in this book), which explains the process and timeframes involved for an academic evaluation.

- Submit the Teacher Referral for Student Evaluation to the appropriate school administrator(s), along with supporting documentation of the Teacher Observation and Parent Observations worksheets.

- Before and during the evaluation process, the teacher will provide additional academic interventions, and will continue to observe and document those results.

- Before and during the evaluation process, the teacher will be an instrumental participant and advocate for the student.

Teachers should not wait for someone else (such as a parent) to refer a student for academic evaluation.

To know that a student is struggling unnecessarily and not take positive action is negligence.

> Note: All forms, in 8 ½" x 11" (letter size), are available with ownership (purchase) of A Child's Touchstone. Go to www.achildstouchstone.com to download them for your use.

Kellie age 10

"If you make listening and observation
your occupation, you will gain
much more than you can by talk."

-Sir Robert Baden-Powell
Founder of the Boy Scouts, 1857-1941

"It is infinitely more useful for a child to hear a story told by a person than by computer. Because the greatest part of the learning experience lies not in the particular words of the story but in the involvement with the individual reading it".

–Frank Smith,
Contemporary psycho-linguistic

Teacher Observations:
Student "Listening Comprehension" Evaluation

STUDENT NAME: _____

GRADE: _____ SUBJECT: _____

TEACHER: _____

Listening comprehension involves phonological processing (expression), process speed, working memory (auditory), long-term memory and executive functioning.

Check the appropriate boxes, using the following rating system:

4 = ALMOST ALWAYS **3** = FREQUENTLY **2** = SOMETIMES **1** = HARDLY EVER

N/A = NOT APPLICABLE TO GRADE LEVEL

	4	3	2	1	N/A
Difficulty counting syllables in a word					
Difficulty with phonemic awareness					
Difficulty with onsetrhyme blending of words					
Difficulty recognizing words that rhyme					
Difficulty linking letters to sounds					

(Continued on the next page)

	4	3	2	1	N/A
Difficulty blending sounds to form real words					
Difficulty recognizing and/or producing rhyming words					
Difficulty singing or reciting short rhymes and songs					
Difficulty blending onsetrhymes to form real words					
Difficulty segmenting, deleting and/or combining sounds in a word					
Difficulty with verbal shortterm memory					
Difficulty with rapid serial naming					
Difficulty with articulation speed					
Lacks phonological processing skills					
Difficulty identifying specific sounds at the beginning, middle and end of words					
Unable to make a new word by replacing a specific sound with another sound					

SCORING: Majority of ratings in columns 3 and 4 suggests DYSLEXIA symptoms.

Teacher Signature: _____ Date: _____

Teacher Observations:
Student "Oral Expression" Evaluation

STUDENT NAME: _____

GRADE: _____ SUBJECT: _____

TEACHER: _____

Oral expression involves motor coordination processing.

Check the appropriate boxes, using the following rating system:

4 = ALMOST ALWAYS **3** = FREQUENTLY **2** = SOMETIMES **1** = HARDLY EVER

N/A = NOT APPLICABLE TO GRADE LEVEL

	4	3	2	1	N/A
Cannot blend sounds					
Guesses words from initial letter					
Reads orally without expression					
Avoids oral reading					
Spends a limited amount of time on reading activities					

(Continued on the next page)

	4	3	2	1	N/A
Reading errors show no connection to the sounds of letters (the word "big" is read as "goat")					
Inability to read common onesyllable words or to sound out words ("mat," "cat," "hop," "nap")					
Stumbles on reading multisyllable words or fails to come close to sounding out the full word					
Reading accuracy is laborious and lacks fluency					
Difficulty manipulating sounds in words ("cat" without the "c" becomes "at," or "line" without the "n" becomes "lie")					

SCORING: Majority of ratings in columns 3 and 4 suggests DYSLEXIA symptoms.

Teacher Signature: _____ Date: _____

Teacher Observations:
Student "Basic Reading Skills" Evaluation

STUDENT NAME: _____

GRADE: _____ SUBJECT: _____

TEACHER: _____

Basic reading skills involve processing speed, auditory or visual (orthographic) processing, working memory and long-term memory.

Check the appropriate boxes, using the following rating system:

4 = ALMOST ALWAYS **3** = FREQUENTLY **2** = SOMETIMES **1** = HARDLY EVER

N/A = NOT APPLICABLE TO GRADE LEVEL

	4	3	2	1	N/A
Does not recall correct order of letters ("fro" instead of "for")					
Misplaces silent "e"					
Difficulty with multisyllable words					
Does not remember variant or unusual spellings					
Unable to retain memory stock of basic spelling words					
Difficulty connecting sounds to letters					

(Continued on the next page)

	4	3	2	1	N/A
Difficulty breaking sounds apart in words when spelling					
Overreliance on auditory features ("becuz" for "because")					
Demonstrates incomplete letter patterns ("both" for "bought")					
Reads at a slow, inaccurate and labored pace					
Unable to identify letters presented at random					
Unable to write the alphabet correctly in sequence					
Unable to recite the alphabet in sequence (without singing or chanting)					
Inability to read common onesyllable words or to sound out words ("mat," "cat," "hop," "nap")					
Unable to read satisfactorily in spite of adequate intelligence and educational opportunity					
Demonstrates consistent letter reversals ("dady" for "baby") (This is an orthographic processing issue)					
Difficulty reading words or recognizing words in isolation					
Difficulty holding information about sounds/words in memory					
Difficulty with spelling					

SCORING: Majority of ratings in columns 3 and 4 suggests DYSLEXIA symptoms.

Teacher Signature: _____ Date: _____

Teacher Observations:
Student "Reading Fluency" Evaluation

STUDENT NAME: _____

GRADE: _____ SUBJECT: _____

TEACHER: _____

Reading fluency involves processing speed, auditory processing/auditory working memory, associative memory and verbal short-term memory.

Check the appropriate boxes, using the following rating system:

4 = ALMOST ALWAYS **3** = FREQUENTLY **2** = SOMETIMES **1** = HARDLY EVER

N/A = NOT APPLICABLE TO GRADE LEVEL

	4	3	2	1	N/A
Difficulty accurately decoding nonsense and unfamiliar words					
Speech is not fluent, uses lots of fillers ("um," "uh," "you know")					
Uses immature speech					
Not fluent at telling stories or giving oral reports					
Difficulty expressing him/herself clearly and fluently					
Processes spoken language more slowly than peers					

(Continued on the next page)

	4	3	2	1	N/A
Uses imprecise language and vague references to "stuff" or "things"					
Difficulty pronouncing long, unfamiliar or complicated words					
Reads slowly with many inaccuracies					
Trouble remembering dates, names or random lists					
Unable to come up with a verbal response quickly when questioned					
Leaves out parts of words or confuses the order of the parts of words					
Difficulty with verbal short-term memory					
Unable to find the exact word, such as confusing words that sound alike (lotion for ocean).					

SCORING: Majority of ratings in columns 3 and 4 suggests DYSLEXIA symptoms.

Teacher Signature: _____ Date: _____

Teacher Observations:
Student "Reading Comprehension" Evaluation

STUDENT NAME: _____

GRADE: _____ SUBJECT: _____

TEACHER: _____

Reading comprehension involves fluid reasoning, morphological awareness and processing speed, working memory, executive functions, sustained attention and successive processing.

Check the appropriate boxes, using the following rating system:

4 = ALMOST ALWAYS **3** = FREQUENTLY **2** = SOMETIMES **1** = HARDLY EVER

N/A = NOT APPLICABLE TO GRADE LEVEL

	4	3	2	1	N/A
Unable to answer questions after reading					
Unable to understand main ideas of a passage					
Unable to recall sequences of written information					
Unable to draw conclusions from a passage					
Unable to read and complete math "story" problems					

(Continued on the next page)

	4	3	2	1	N/A
Unable to remember what was just read					
Reliance on context to discern the meaning of what is read					
Studies for a test but forgets what was learned					
Difficulty shifting focus from one task to another					
Difficulty with total recall of information without a cue					
Difficulty with essay questions on tests					
Difficulty with short-term memory					
Difficulty with long-term memory					
Skips questions, misses questions or leaves them blank					
Loses place while working on reading assignments					
Possesses a better ability to understand words in context than to read isolated single words					
Possesses a high level of understanding when read to					

SCORING: Majority of ratings in columns 3 and 4 suggests DYSLEXIA symptoms

Teacher Signature: _____ Date: _____

Teacher Observations:
Student "Written Expression" Evaluation

STUDENT NAME: _____

GRADE: _____ SUBJECT: _____

TEACHER: _____

Written expression involves orthographic processing, oral expression, fluid reasoning, working memory, executive functions (planning, organizing), motor coordination and phonological awareness.

Check the appropriate boxes, using the following rating system:

4 = ALMOST ALWAYS **3** = FREQUENTLY **2** = SOMETIMES **1** = HARDLY EVER

N/A = NOT APPLICABLE TO GRADE LEVEL

	4	3	2	1	N/A
Forgets how letters look					
Difficulty remembering basic sight words					
Confuses letters with similar appearance ("n" for "h")					
Difficulty copying from a book or classroom board to paper					
Misreads little words in text ("were" for "where")					

(Continued on the next page)

	4	3	2	1	N/A
Spells the same word in different ways					
Confuses letters when spelling ("b" for "d")					
Spells words how they sound, rather than how they look					
Confuses letters in words when reading ("on" for "no")					
Has a tendency to miss middle letters when reading					
Difficulty learning how to form letters					
Spells phonetically					
Difficulty staying on the line when writing					
Poor organization on the page					
Excessive erasures, especially due to faulty form					
Overall writing effort is awkward or uneven					
Writing resembles "bird scratching"					
Writing, for the most part, is illegible					
Difficulty distinguishing between capital and lowercase letters					
School work deteriorates toward the end of the writing exercise					

(Continued on the next page)

	4	3	2	1	N/A
Constructs sentences poorly (syntax)					
Many misspellings					
Poor spacing between words and sentences					
Uses capital and lowercase letters incorrectly					
Leaves out words when writing					
Makes many grammatical errors					
Makes many punctuation errors					
Spells the same word several different ways					
Misuse of homophones					
Difficulty with orthographic processing					
Written word does not reflect his/her potential					
Unusual difficulty with handwriting					
Difficulty completing written assignments					
Marks from bottom to top when forming certain letters and numbers					
Composes meaningful content in spite of poor handwriting and spelling					

(Continued on the next page)

	4	3	2	1	N/A
Demonstrates minimal problem with words that make phonemic sense ("grand") but has significant problems with words that don't (such as "right")					

SCORING: Majority of ratings in columns 3 and 4 suggests DYSLEXIA symptoms.

Teacher Signature: _____ Date: _____

Teacher Observations:
Student "Math Computation" Evaluation

STUDENT NAME: _____

GRADE: _____ SUBJECT: _____

TEACHER: _____

Math computation involves processing speed, working memory and long-term memory/associative memory.

Check the appropriate boxes, using the following rating system:

4 = ALMOST ALWAYS **3** = FREQUENTLY **2** = SOMETIMES **1** = HARDLY EVER

N/A = NOT APPLICABLE TO GRADE LEVEL

	4	3	2	1	N/A
Difficulty with simple counting					
Confusion of similar-looking mathematical signs					
Confusion with number orders (units, tens, hundreds)					
Difficulty remembering shapes of numbers					
Confusion with similar-looking numbers					
Difficulty learning sequences (times table, days of week, months of year)					
Difficulty with one-to-one correspondence between numbers, symbols and items/objects					

(Continued on the next page)

	4	3	2	1	N/A
Unable to remember order of mathematical operations					
Slow speed of processing, computation and answer retrieval					
Confusion between greater than and less than					
Difficulty counting backwards (10, 9, 8 and so on)					
Unable to perform simple cognitive tasks quickly					
Unable to calculate and perform basic operations quickly					
Difficulty remembering numbers or skipping numbers					
Difficulty recalling basic math facts (2 + 4 = 6)					
Uses fingers to count instead of using other strategies					
Difficulty writing numbers clearly					
Difficulty putting numbers in the correct column					
Difficulty telling time with an analog clock					
Struggles to connect numbers to reallife situations, such knowing that "3" can apply to any group that has three things in it—3 cookies, 3 cars, 3 kids, etc.					

SCORING: Majority of ratings in columns 3 and 4 suggests DYSLEXIA symptoms.

Teacher Signature: _____ Date: _____

Teacher Observations:
Student "Math Reasoning/Problem Solving" Evaluation

STUDENT NAME: _____

GRADE: _____ SUBJECT: _____

TEACHER: _____

Math problem solving involves fluid reasoning—applying prior knowledge to new situations. Fluid reasoning involves inductive and deductive reasoning.

Check the appropriate boxes, using the following rating system:

4 = ALMOST ALWAYS **3** = FREQUENTLY **2** = SOMETIMES **1** = HARDLY EVER

N/A = NOT APPLICABLE TO GRADE LEVEL

	4	3	2	1	N/A
Difficulty showing all steps to a math problem					
Requires more time to solve math problems					
Needs to re-read a math problem several times before understanding what is being asked					
Difficulties applying prior knowledge to new problems					
Difficulty seeing relationships between prior and new information					

(Continued on the next page)

	4	3	2	1	N/A
Trouble measuring, like ingredients in a simple recipe					
Difficulty grasping information on graphs or charts					
Difficulty estimating speed and distance					
Difficulty finding different approaches to the same math problem					
Difficulty with money matters, estimating the total costs, and making change					
Difficulty navigating through mathematical problems					
Difficulty with concept of distance and measurement					
Difficulty performing simple tasks, such as daily expense calculations, higher financial planning and budgeting					
Poor sense of mathematical concepts, rules, formulas and sequences					
Difficulty coming up with a plan to solve a math problem					
Difficulty forming and recognizing logical relationships among mathematical patterns					

SCORING: Majority of ratings in columns 3 and 4 suggests DYSLEXIA symptoms.

Teacher Signature: _____ Date: _____

Teacher Observations:
Student "Productivity" Evaluation

STUDENT NAME: _____

GRADE: _____ SUBJECT: _____

TEACHER: _____

Check the appropriate boxes, using the following rating system:

4 = ALMOST ALWAYS **3** = FREQUENTLY **2** = SOMETIMES **1** = HARDLY EVER

N/A = NOT APPLICABLE TO GRADE LEVEL

	4	3	2	1
Participates in large group class discussion				
Participates in small group class discussion				
Follows/remembers directions without prompting				
Keeps pace/follows along when reading with class				
Keeps track of and remembers supplies needed for task				
Finishes independent work within assigned time				
Completes all school work assigned on time				
Completes and turns in "in-class" work on time				

(Continued on the next page)

	4	3	2	1
Written work is legible and neat				
Takes tests carefully and completes within time allowed				
Turns in all assigned homework when due				
Concentrates on task at hand				
School work is organized and in proper order				
Follows class rules				
Follows through and completes work on group projects				
Plans well and uses time wisely to accomplish tasks/goals				
Is comfortable asking teacher for guidance when needed				
Compares favorably in overall productivity with average student in class				

SCORING: Majority of ratings in columns 1 and 2 suggest, SUBSTANTIAL interference in learning.

Teacher Signature: _____ Date: _____

Teacher Referral for Student Evaluation: Submission Sheet

(Page 1 of 3)

STUDENT NAME: _____ I.D. # _____

D.O.B. _____ GRADE: _____ GENDER: _____

SCHOOL: _____

REFERRING TEACHER: _____

PARENT(S)/GUARDIAN(S): _____

Check **areas of concern** as reason for referral:

Academic Performance:
(check all that apply and attach corresponding Teacher Evaluation Report for each area of concern)

___ Listening comprehension
___ Oral expression
___ Basic reading skills
___ Reading fluency
___ Reading comprehension
___ Written expression
___ Math computation
___ Math reasoning/problem solving

Language Arts:
(areas of concern—check all that apply)

___ Alphabetic knowledge
___ Phonemic awareness
___ Reading comprehension
___ Reading fluency
___ Writing conventions
___ Written expression
___ Written mechanics
___ Vocabulary (reading/oral)
___ Word identification
___ Other: _____

Student Name: _____

Teacher Referral for Student Evaluation: Submission Sheet

Mathematics:
(areas of concern—check all that apply)

__ Analysis
__ Basic math facts
__ Computation
__ Geometry or algebra (circle)
__ Math reasoning
__ Measurement
__ Memory/remembering
__ Probability/data
__ Problem solving
__ Word problems
__ Other: _____

Communication:
(areas of concern—check all that apply)

__ Articulation
__ Communicate basic needs and wants
__ Expressive language
__ Fluency
__ Knowledge of soundletter association
__ Receptive knowledge/language
__ Other: _____

General Intelligence:
(areas of concern—check all that apply)

__ Applying knowledge
__ Comparing/contrasting ideas of objects
__ Interpreting data to make decisions
__ Memory
__ Perceptual discrimination
__ Predicting events or results
__ Problem solving
__ Other: _____

Student Name: _____

Teacher Referral for Student Evaluation: Submission Sheet

Work Skills, Study Skills, Technical and Vocational Functioning:

(areas of concern—check all that apply <u>and</u> attach corresponding Teacher Observations, Student Productivity Evaluation)

__ Attending to tasks
__ Completing school work
__ Following instructions/directions
__ Independent work habits
__ Organizing materials/belongings
__ Other: _____

Current Grade:

(complete all that apply)

Reading	
Writing	
Spelling	
English	
Science	
Social Studies	
History	
Mathematics	
Other:	

The following supporting documentation is attached hereto:

1)_____
2)_____
3)_____
4)_____

Referring Teacher's Signature: _____ Date: _____

Received by authorized school personnel:

Name: _____

Signature: _____ Date: _____

Student Name: _____

"Strength lies in differences,
not in similarities."

-Stephen Covey (1932- 2012),
American educator and author

Evelyn age 12

"Anyone can give up; it's the easiest
thing in the world to do. But to
hold it together when everyone
else would understand if you fell
apart, that's true strength."

-Christopher Reeves
Actor, 1952-2004

CHAPTER 17

Parent Referral for Student Evaluation

Most parents assume that schools are responsible for identifying and referring students for evaluation for a possible learning disability. In a perfect world, this would be true.

The reality is that most schools lack the necessary ability and resources to fulfill the "Child Find" law. This leaves an unacceptable gap in locating students who need special education services.

The solution is for parents to become more informed on what their child's education rights are and how they can advocate for them when the school is less engaged in Child Find activities.

Parents know when their child is struggling in school, because they begin to feel powerless to help them. This is the beginning of much frustration, anxiety and fear. This is also when parents need to step up, get involved, become informed and expect support and results from their child's school.

When parents observe academic struggles in their child, they need to form an "action plan" that includes the following:

- Arrange a face-to-face meeting with their child's teacher(s).

- Prior to the meeting, the parent(s) should complete the Parent Observations worksheet(s) (included in this book. For example, if the child is in fourth grade, parent(s) should complete the Parent Observations worksheets for early childhood (first five years), first and second grade, as well as third and fourth grade. This is because symptoms of dyslexia accumulate and move forward in the child's life. The accumulation of symptoms documents the patterns of dyslexia. A copy of the Parent Observations worksheets should be provided to the teacher(s).

- Prior to the meeting, ask the teacher(s) to complete the Teacher Observations worksheets (included in this book), covering the areas of Listening Comprehension, Oral Expression, Basic Reading Skills, Reading Fluency, Reading Comprehension, Written Expression, Math Computation, Math Reasoning/Problem Solving and Student Productivity. These worksheets are designed for easy completion and understanding and will assist teacher(s) and parent(s) while discussing the student's challenges and strengths. Parents should request a copy of the completed Teacher Observations worksheets prior to their meeting.

- During the meeting, parents should review and discuss, for clarification, the Teacher Observations and Parent Observations worksheets. This is an opportunity for parent(s) and teacher(s) to learn more about the student, on both an academic and personal level.

- Bring student work samples to the meeting that are of concern. Teachers review and grade a lot of assignments and may not have any current examples of completed work.

- Parents should be prepared to request that their child be referred for evaluation for a possible learning disability. Parents should have a prepared letter (a sample letter is included in this book) requesting such a referral, and give it to the teacher at the meeting. The teacher will be obligated by law to submit the referral request to the appropriate school administrators to begin the process. Parents should have the teacher sign an extra copy of the letter, acknowledging receipt of the letter of referral.

- Parents should not accept any alternative interventions in lieu of having their child evaluated. Teachers are not prohibited from offering additional educational support and/or accommodations, prior to or during the evaluation process. If the teacher hasn't already provided additional support or accommodations, there's no need to wait until they do. A struggling student does not gain from the luxury of someone else's time schedule.

- Parents should be clear as to their expectations of the school to evaluate their child within the legal timeframes. The teacher(s) and school need to know the parents are well informed and will take any action necessary to advocate for their child.

- Parents should create a student documentation binder for their records. The binder should contain all written communications (including email), school documentation and letters, student work samples, any private evaluations/assessment reports, Teacher and Parent Observations worksheets, progress reports and report cards, teacher implemented interventions or accommodations (if any), and any documented/recording of meetings.

- Parents should keep the lines of communicate open with the student's teacher(s), prior, during and after academic evaluation. Their support and advocacy is critical.

Parents should not wait for someone else, such as a teacher, to refer their child for academic evaluation.

To know that a child is unnecessarily struggling academically and not take action is negligence.

Note: All forms, in 8 ½" x 11" (letter size), are available with ownership (purchase) of A Child's Touchstone. Go to www.achildstouchstone.com to download them for your use.

Parent(s) Requesting Referral for Evaluation

SAMPLE LETTER

Parent Name
Street Address, City, State, Zip Code
Telephone Number

Date

Name of School
Street Address
City, State, Zip Code

Attention: Name of Principal

Re: Name of Student and Current Grade
Request/Referral for Educational Evaluation

Dear Name of Principal:

I am writing to you because Name of Student is experiencing academic difficulties in school and is struggling to keep up.

Attached is documentation completed by my child's teacher(s) with regards to their observations of Name of Student in the areas of listening comprehension, oral expression, basic reading skills, reading fluency, reading comprehension, written expression, math computation and math reasoning and student productivity.

Accordingly, I hereby request that Name of Student be evaluated for a possible learning disability, in accordance with Child Find obligations of the Individuals with Disabilities Act (IDEA) and Section 504 of the Rehabilitation Act of 1973. I understand there are specific timeframes which we must be followed once a referral and/or request is made, and look forward to receiving confirmation that the time clock and procedures for evaluation have begun.
Thank you for your time and assistance.

Respectfully,   Receipt of Letter

Name and Signature of Parent   by: _____

cc: Name of Teacher(s)   date: _____

Parent Observations:
Early Childhood (First Five Years)

NAME OF CHILD/
STUDENT: _____

AGE: _____   SCHOOL: _____

	Yes	No
Dyslexia is in the family genes		
Prone to ear infections		
Late crawling or walking		
Difficulty learning to tie shoelaces		
Difficulty fastening buttons and/or getting dressed		
Ambidextrous (or late establishing a dominant hand)		
Delayed speech—mispronounces words		
Mixes pronunciation sounds of multi-syllable words		
Confuses directional words (right vs. left, before vs. after)		
Difficulty remember/memorizing the names of letters or sounds in the alphabet, or letters in name		
Difficulty remembering home address, telephone number, date of birth and/or last name		

(Continued on the next page)

	Yes	No
Difficulty naming familiar objects, colors, letters of alphabet		
Bed wetting after age four		
Extra deep sleeper		
Seems irritated or anxious in noisy environments		
Difficulty following more than one instruction at a time		
Difficulty recognizing rhyming patterns, such as cat, bat, cat		
Difficulty expressing ideas or thoughts, unable to recall the right word, often pausing and using "um" or "like" to fill in the blanks		
Difficulty catching, kicking or throwing a ball		
Difficulty understanding humor, puns or jokes		
Can seem clumsy, dropping, spilling or knocking things over		
Confuses similar-looking letters and/or numbers		
Does not detect or respond properly to teasing		
Difficulty picking up on people's moods or feelings		

Parent Signature: _____ Date: _____

Parent Observations:
First and Second Grade

NAME OF CHILD/
STUDENT: _____

GRADE: _____ SCHOOL: _____

	Yes	No
Often loses place while reading		
Lacks fluency while reading, often pausing midsentence		
Recognizes a word in one sentence but not in the next		
Often repeats reading mistakes over and over		
Difficulty "getting to the point"		
Struggles with uneven printing, spacing between letters and words and staying on the line		
Confuses similar-looking words, letters and/or numbers		
Trouble telling time with an analog clock		
Frequently mispronounces words; reads phonetically		
Guesses or substitutes words while reading		
Difficulty copying/writing notes		

(Continued on the next page)

	Yes	No
Difficulty working independently without redirection		
Does not enjoy reading for pleasure		
Often loses things		
Has difficulty retelling what was just said or read		
Inconsistent spelling (whether correct or not)		
Difficulty learning/memorizing basic addition and subtraction facts		
Difficulty remembering new vocabulary words		
Struggles with comprehension of ideas and thoughts		
Forgetful in daily and routine activities		

Parent Signature: _____   Date: _____

NOTE:

It is also important to complete "Parent Observations in Early Childhood" and include it with this form, "Parent Observations for First and Second Grade."

If your child is showing signs and symptoms in first or second grade, they most likely showed symptoms in early childhood. Many symptoms of dyslexia accumulate and move forward in the child's life. It is important to document "patterns" of dyslexic symptoms

Parent Observations:
Third and Fourth Grade

NAME OF CHILD/
STUDENT: _____

GRADE: _____ SCHOOL: _____

	Yes	No
Difficulty organizing homework assignments and due dates		
Cannot remember/memorize oral multiple instructions		
Writing/printing is messy and incomplete		
Substitutes or omits words entirely when writing		
Difficulty proofing and self-correcting homework		
Difficulty organizing home responsibilities, tasks and activities		
Misuses words in conversation		
Avoids reading, claiming tiredness		
Graded homework does not return home		
Homework to be completed goes missing		

(Continued on the next page)

	Yes	No
Has limited interest in books without pictures		
Difficulty understanding concepts of time		
Difficulty understanding concepts of money		
Throws away poorly graded assignments and tests before they reach home		
Has lied about homework being turned in—saying it got lost		
Does not want to complete daily homework—says it's too hard		
Experiences bullying by peers, including teasing, laughing and name calling.		
Is sometimes upset and does not want to go to school		

Parent Signature: _____   Date: _____

NOTE:

It is also important to complete "Parent Observations in Early Childhood" and "Parent Observations for First and Second Grade," and include them with this form, "Parent Observations for Third and Fourth Grade."

If your child is showing signs and symptoms in third and fourth grade, they most likely showed symptoms in early childhood through second grade. Many symptoms of dyslexia accumulate and move forward in the child's life. It is important to document "patterns" of dyslexic symptoms.

Parent Observations:
Fifth and Sixth Grade

NAME OF CHILD/
STUDENT: _____

GRADE: _____   SCHOOL: _____

	Yes	No
Does not enjoy reading		
Vocabulary is limited and vague		
Avoids or is reluctant to engage in tasks that require sustained mental effort, such as homework		
Performs inconsistently on home tasks or responsibilities		
Has a poor sense of direction		
Is disorganized; poor at planning for future tests or assignments		
Unable to remember names of people, places, things and dates		
Difficulty managing multiple tasks at the same time, especially if instructions are presented in multiple ways		
Feeling overwhelmed, unable to complete tasks on time		
Lying about homework to be completed		

(Continued on the next page)

	Yes	No
Experiencing intensified bullying by peers		
Being accused by teachers of not working to potential		
Becoming uninterested in attending school		
Overall grades are slipping		

Parent Signature: _____   Date: _____

NOTE:

It is also important to complete "Parent Observations in Early Childhood," "Parent Observations for First and Second Grade" and Parent Observations for Third and Fourth Grade," and include them with this form, "Parent Observations for Fifth and Sixth Grade."

If your child is showing signs and symptoms in fifth and sixth grade, they most likely showed symptoms in early childhood through fourth grade. Many symptoms of dyslexia accumulate and move forward in the child's life. It is important to document "patterns" of dyslexic symptoms.

Parent Observations:
Seventh and Eighth Grade

NAME OF CHILD/
STUDENT: _____

GRADE: _____   SCHOOL: _____

	Yes	No
Poor study skills and time management		
Difficulty learning a second language		
Poor note taking and outlining strategies for tests		
Difficulty discriminating between words with multiple meanings		
Difficulties communicating or understanding what is said		
Unable to remember what was just read		
Uninterested in reading		
Incomplete homework		
Difficulties with mathematics, order of operations or multiple steps		
Bullying by peers and others continues and is intensified		

(Continued on the next page)

	Yes	No
Written work has many spelling errors, is incomplete and is too brief		
Prefers to print rather than write in cursive		
Poor short-term memory; difficulties remembering previously taught knowledge and their instructions		
Failing grades		
Frustration by teachers that the student is not working hard enough, is not motivated and is not living up to potential		

Parent Signature: _____ Date: _____

NOTE:

It is also important to complete "Parent Observations in Early Childhood," "Parent Observations for First and Second Grade," "Parent Observations for Third and Fourth Grade" and "Parent Observations for Fifth and Sixth Grade" and include them with this form, "Parent Observations for Seventh and Eighth Grade."

If your child is showing signs and symptoms in seventh and eighth grade, they most likely showed symptoms in early childhood through sixth grade. Many symptoms of dyslexia accumulate and move forward in the child's life. It is important to document "patterns" of dyslexic symptoms.

Parent Observations
Ninth Through Twelfth Grade

NAME OF CHILD/
STUDENT: _____

GRADE: _____   SCHOOL: _____

	Yes	No
Struggles completing homework		
Difficulty remembering multiple-step directions		
Experiences tremendous stress and fatigue during test taking		
Difficulty with oral presentations		
Substantial difficulties mastering mathematical facts		
Limited vocabulary and communication with peers/adults		
Slow reading speed, well below grade level		
Unable to comprehend/remember what is read		
Unable to remember what has been studied for a test		
Unable to remember order of operations in mathematics		
Extremely poor written expression		

(Continued on the next page)

	Yes	No
Large discrepancy between verbal & written communications		
Feels anxious and frustrated; overwhelmed by multiple tasks		
Does not feel prepared during academic testing		
Does not enjoy reading; finds it grueling and exhausting		
Sees self as a poor learner		
Has a lack of confidence and low self-esteem		
Hesitant taking risks involving individual projects, choosing instead simple, less challenging topics or tasks		
Has a poor ability for navigation and sense of direction		
Weak problem solving/coping skills		
Is depressed or has feelings of sadness		
Difficulty making friends; poor social judgment		
Poor grades in most class subjects		
Wants to quit school		

Parent Signature: _____ Date: _____

NOTE:

It is also important to complete "Parent Observations in Early Childhood," "Parent Observations for First and Second Grade," "Parent Observations for Third and Fourth Grade," "Parent Observations for Fifth and Sixth Grade" and "Parent Observations for Seventh and Eighth Grade," and include them with this form, "Parent Observations for Ninth through Twelfth Grade."

If your child is showing signs and symptoms in ninth through twelfth grade, they most likely showed symptoms in early childhood through eighth grade. Many symptoms of dyslexia accumulate and move forward in the child's life. It is important to document "patterns" of dyslexic symptoms.

Bradley age 13

"There is time and hope if we
combine patience with courage."

-Winston Churchill, 1875-1965
Prime Minister of the United Kingdom,
1940-1945 and 1951-1955

CHAPTER 18

Timeline for Special Education Referral, Evaluation and Implementation

Referral Request for Evaluation

Parents, teachers, school administrators, pediatricians, medical specialists, juvenile justice agencies, child and health service agencies, and others providing education and related services can refer a child for evaluation for a suspected learning disability. In all cases, certain protocols must be followed:

- The parent(s) prepare a written letter to the school/school district (see sample letter included in this book) requesting their child be evaluated for a possible learning disability. The letter should include the completed Teacher Observations worksheets (included in this book) from the child's teacher(s). Requests for evaluation should be hand-delivered to the school and acknowledged by the receiving school administrator by signing and dating receipt and providing a copy to the parent(s) for their records.

- Within 15 calendar days from receipt of letter requesting an evaluation, the school must acknowledge the referral request, and provide a consent form for evaluation.

- Within the next 15 calendar days from parental receipt of the consent form for evaluation, parent(s) must sign, date and return the consent form to the school, as addressed.

- The time clock on completing the evaluation process begins when the school (district) acknowledges receipt of the consent to evaluate.

Evaluation

Within the next 60 calendar days, the school special education team must evaluate the student and determine eligibility for special education services and/or accommodations.

- During this 60-day timeframe, the special education team will determine which assessment components/tests will be used and whether any speech, vision, hearing or medical assessments should also be conducted.

- Parent(s) should request, in writing, the names/types of evaluation tests, in order to make sure they are appropriate for identifying dyslexia and the child's learning difficulties. The wrong assessments/tests will result in the wrong diagnosis/evaluation determination.

- Parent(s) will/should be notified as to when evaluation testing will take place, including classroom observation(s).

- Observations must be completed in the student's learning environment, including the classroom, in order to document the student's academic performance.

- Parents are encouraged to be in attendance during these times, even if being present means being outside the evaluation room or classroom.

Individual Education Plan and Implementation

- Upon determining that the student is eligible for special education services, the school team has an additional 30 calendar days in which to develop the Individual Education Plan (IEP).

- Within this 30-day period, the parents are invited to attend an IEP meeting. Evaluation testing results are discussed.

- IEP educational services are outlined and approved.

- Parent(s) sign consent to the IEP.

- Implementation of the IEP begins soon after (usually within 30 days) the parent(s) sign consent to the IEP.

The entire referral, evaluation and IEP implementation process can take up to 120 calendar days. It is important to begin the referral and evaluation process early in the school year. Waiting too long can push completion well into six or seven months when school breaks are included.

Some schools require teachers to issue pre-referral requests before recommending a formal referral for evaluation. Pre-referrals are not part of any law. The "pre-referral doctrine" was created by some well-intended, yet misled school officials who believed a formal referral could be avoided by simply offering classroom interventions that, in their opinion, had not yet been offered by the classroom teacher. No offense, but who are they to decide what interventions a teacher has or has not applied?

Most teachers give it their all… and then some. If a teacher believes that a student needs to be evaluated for a learning disability, then nothing will convince me otherwise.

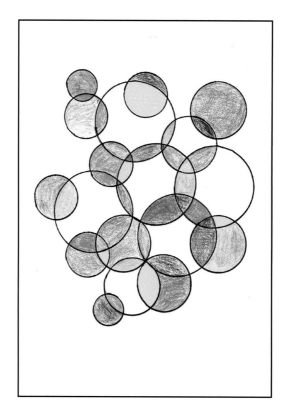

Cody age 10

"In chess, knowledge is a very
transient thing. It changes so fast
that even a single mouse-slip
sometimes changes the evaluation."

-Viswanathan Anand
Chess Grandmaster

CHAPTER 19

Evaluation Testing
for Identification of Dyslexia

Parents may be surprised to learn that school related evaluations for specific learning disabilities do not always include testing for dyslexia. This is because most school psychologists, paraprofessionals, educational specialists and the like, do not hold the required professional certifications in order to conduct this testing.

School evaluations typically focus on student weaknesses while learning in an academic environment within the guidelines of the "specific learning disability" category.

Although some educators have knowledge on dyslexia, the majority lack training on teaching to dyslexic students. This is why so many dyslexic children are undiagnosed, misdiagnosed or not provided the correct educational supports.

Knowing that school educators/administrators lack specific knowledge on dyslexia, parents might consider having their child assessed by a credentialed professional who can provide valuable information to the school evaluation.

A school evaluation is not exclusive to just their findings, but must include observations by parents/family members, and any evaluations, assessments and diagnosis reports by credentialed professionals on dyslexia.

Appropriate testing for signs and symptoms of dyslexia should include components of expressive or receptive oral language, expressive or receptive written language, intellectual functioning, cognitive processing and educational achievement.

It is important to be informed of the numerous types of testing currently available for dyslexia symptoms. It is then up to parents, special education educators and medical professionals to decide which ones work best.

Worldwide, hundreds of tests are available for determining a learning disability, but testing is only as good as the knowledge and training of the tester. If the tester lacks education on dyslexia, the tests results will be compromised, inaccurate and incomplete. Parents should not assume that school provided educational evaluation testing is current and all-inclusive when determining a learning disability such as dyslexia.

Although the number of tests available may seem overwhelming, it's important to know they exist. While it's impossible to list them all, the following is a short list of tests used in determining dyslexia characteristics:

- Boston Naming Test

- Comprehensive Test of Phonological Processing (CTOPP)

- Decoding Skills Test (DST)

- Diagnostic Achievement Battery

- Dyslexia Screening Instrument (DSI)

- Gray Oral Reading Tests (GORT)

- Stanford Binet Intelligence Scale

- Stanford Binet Memory for Sentences Test

- Test of Auditory Analysis Skills (TAAS)

- Test of Awareness of Language Segments (TALS)

- Test of Memory and Learning (TOMAL)

- Test of Word Reading Efficiency (TOWRE)

- Wide Range Achievement Test in Reading (WRAT-R)

- Woodcock Johnson Cognitive Abilities Test

- Word Identification and Attack Test (WIAT)

- Word Identification and Spelling Test (WIST)

In addition to the preceding tests, the International Dyslexia Association (www.eida.org) has listed several commonly used measurements for the identification of dyslexia. A link to the IDA can be found on my website, along with the organization's testing fact sheet.

Depending on the age of the child, some tests may be more appropriate than others. An evaluation for suspicion of dyslexia can take place at any age, but the earlier the better. Children as early as age three, when appropriately evaluated, can indicate possible symptoms of dyslexia.

Before a school evaluation is performed, parents should be asking what tests will be administered and whether additional tests recommended by the student's medical professional will be included.

Incomplete evaluations can result in incorrect educational support, therapies and accommodations, including denial of services. And because many school evaluators lack in depth knowledge of dyslexia, they may not know how to interpret the results or what school/academic accommodations are most effective.

The school process used for evaluating a student for a learning disability does not have the same urgency or expectancy as that of the child's parents. Some disadvantages of school-performed evaluations include:

Waiting for the child to fail before referring them for evaluation.

- Lack of teacher training on dyslexia, which leads to ignorance and no help for the struggling dyslexic student.

- Misdiagnosis for another health impairment unrelated to dyslexia.

- Reports that do not provide enough detailed information on the child's underlying cognitive difficulties because the assessment instruments used for evaluation are inadequate and incomplete.

- Inappropriate or incomplete recommendations for educational support and accommodations for the dyslexic student.

Parents must be pro-active in navigating through the evaluation maze and not completely rely on school personnel to make all the right decisions. To be knowledgeable and empowered, one must be well informed.

"Our prime purpose in this life is to help others. And if you can't help them, at least don't hurt them."

-Dalai Lama

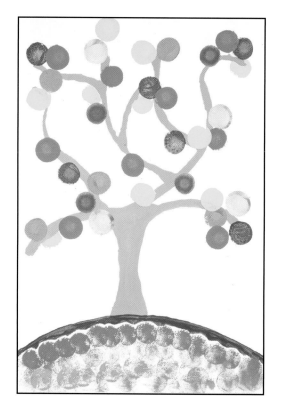

Anderson age 10

"Never take someone's feelings
for granted because you never
know how much courage that
took to show it to you."

-Anonymous

CHAPTER 20

Role of the School Psychologist

School psychologists wear many hats. They provide counseling in various areas involving student life, evaluate students for eligibility for special education services, collaborate with teachers and parents in developing action plans to improve academic performance, provide appropriate referrals regarding vocational needs of students, and document everything, to name a few.

School psychologists face tremendous demands that are difficult to fulfill. For some school districts, the student to school psychologist ratio could be five hundred to one. Which is why it can take several months before a student receives services. In fact, the number of school psychologists is not able or reasonable in establishing productive results.

Currently, school psychologists hold sole responsibility for evaluating students for a possible learning disability and recommending necessary academic supports and services. Lacking is the need for classroom teachers to be trained on dyslexia, including how to correctly implement teaching methods specific to the needs of the dyslexic student. Appropriate training on dyslexia for teachers is crucial. Without training, teachers are left to "wing it", often leading to frustration which can negatively impact the dyslexic student.

Children with dyslexia can qualify for special education services. However, most school psychologists do not hold the appropriate credentials to diagnose dyslexia. Instead, their focus is evaluating students for possible disabilities that negatively affect academic learning. For example - If a dyslexic student is found not eligible for special education services, it does not mean the student doesn't have dyslexia. It means the school psychologist's evaluation did not find a disability that negatively affects academic performance, and instead believes the student is functioning academically at an average rate as other students.

If this occurs and the parent(s) do not agree with the school psychologist's analysis, a private, comprehensive evaluation and assessment by a clinical psycho-educational expert or pediatric neuropsychologist, is the next step. Their knowledge of dyslexia and professional diagnosis will be beneficial in determining educational support and services needed for the dyslexic child, when appealing the school's decision.

Some schools insist they're not allowed to identify students as dyslexic from a school evaluation, because they believe the word "dyslexia" is indicative of a medical diagnosis. And although there are no laws that confirm this position, some suggest that these schools avoid using the term "dyslexia", because doing so may require them to provide methodology specific to a learning disability they may not be trained on providing.

There are however, many schools that have in place, trained educators and professionals that diagnose dyslexia, and able to provide programs and services specific to dyslexic students. They believe that dyslexia is a "specific" definition that deserves specific attention.

With this knowledge, parents need to be vigilant in navigating evaluations and academic support for their child. Children with dyslexia do not have the luxury of time when their learning experience is in the hands of those who may not have the appropriate training to help them.

"How far you go in life depends on your being tender with the young, compassionate with the aged, sympathetic with the striving and tolerant of the weak and strong. Because someday in life you will have been all of these."

- George Washington Carver
(1860 - 1943), Inventor

Elizabeth age 15

"Hugs can do great amounts of
good, especially for children."

-Princess Diana
Princess of Whales, 1961-1997

CHAPTER 21

Role of the Pediatrician

Parents take their child to the pediatrician for an annual checkup. The child's weight and height are measured, and vision and hearing are tested. The pediatrician will also ask questions about the child's educational progress. Quite often however, the questions are too vague for dependable answers.

Asking a parent how well the child is doing school is too open-ended. One parent's idea of doing well in school could mean receiving straight A's and nothing less, while another parent may think that getting C's is good.

The answer from both parents might be "fine" or "not so well," yet neither one of them is really sure and/or correct. In reality, grades have little to do with a child's overall ability and whether they need education support services. Most parents are not aware that an "A" student may still have a need for educational support, the same as a struggling-to-keep-up "C" student. Unfortunately, some schools view average to good grades as a sign that the student does not need educational support. They are wrong.

Unless pediatricians probe further into a child's educational progress, most will not detect any type of learning disability and simply believe everything stated by the parent(s) as gospel. This is a mistake that a 15 minute doctor's appointment cannot afford. And since most parents are not knowledgeable on the signs and symptoms of a learning disability, they rely heavily on the family physician or pediatrician to guide them.

Completing medical and developmental questionnaires ahead of the appointment is important, yet rarely do those documents concentrate on questions specific to possible educational learning disabilities that you cannot see (such as dyslexia). Those questionnaires are a mixed bag, covering everything from drug addiction during pregnancy to a child's obsessive interest in television programming.

In order to help parents and their child, medical questionnaires should cover such additional areas of concern as are specifically related to reading, writing, mathematics, short-term working memory, organization, delayed speech, bed wetting, directional confusion, difficulty expressing thoughts and ideas, proneness to ear infections, difficulties following more than one direction at a time and whether dyslexia is in the family genes. Most parents are open to disclosing these difficulties, if asked in a non-threatening way.

As the child's first line of defense, further evaluation by a pediatric neuropsychologist or other medical professional may become necessary. Referrals for further evaluation use professional knowledge of learning disabilities and are not determined by school grades alone.

Family physicians and pediatricians have extremely important functions in acting as a medical home for their young patients, which includes being vigilant in looking for signs of dyslexia. This book can be a guide.

"Have a heart that never hardens, a temper that never tires, a touch that never hurts."

-Charles Dickens (1812 - 1870),
English writer

Electra age 12

"It is paradoxical that many educators and parents still differentiate between a time for learning and a time for play without seeing the vital connection between them."

-Leo F. Buscaglia
Author and Professor

CHAPTER 22

Parent(s) versus Teacher(s)

Parents and teachers often disagree on approaches to learning. Teachers are trained on teaching methods and curriculum, but not necessarily on ways of teaching to different learning styles. Parents are intimately aware of their child's habits, attitude and ways they learn but not necessarily how it translates to academic learning.

If children had the same teacher from kindergarten through twelfth grade, common ground and understanding between the teacher and parents would probably be excellent.

If teachers had the same education and same quality training on teaching to different learning styles, at all grade levels, then student learning and teacher/parent collaboration would be outstanding.

If parents were more knowledgeable on their child's learning style and empowered to make positive changes that support learning-style differences, millions of children would benefit.

Sadly, most parent/teacher relationships do not include a democracy with a level playing field. Most teachers and school administrators believe they are the ultimate authority on education, and parents believe they are the ultimate authority on what's best for their child. If either side is more powerful, it's called a dictatorship.

Schools spend millions of taxpayer dollars "lawyering up" to defend allegations of educational neglect of students. Parents spend the same, trying to recover tutoring costs and other services they believe should be provided by the school. Both sides believe they've been wronged, and the child is stuck in the middle, trying to learn, while dodging parent/teacher daggers. It's time to press the pause button.

It's worth noting that the responsibility to educate our children lies solely with parents or adults within their care. To assist parents, professional educators offer services to support academic learning. The majority of educators are compensated by the community of taxpayers served.

In most communities, the quality of education provided is completely dependent upon the decisions of those offering the services. And while minimum educational standards are required, interpretation of education implementation and compliance is broad and varied.

For these reasons, educators and parents often butt heads and disagree as to how children should be taught. Educational supports for children with learning disabilities are also often contentious.

Accountability is important. If parents are accountable for their children and professional educators are accountable for their students, why are there so many conflicts between parents and teachers? Maybe it's because parents and teachers blame each other for not doing what they believe to be their jobs.

Like all partnerships, positive parent-teacher relationship is critical to the success of the child/student. It is important that parents and teachers understand their individual roles and responsibilities, and not try to pass them on to each other. If this occurs, permanent wedges of resentment and friction will develop, and the adults in the room will be reduced to childlike squabbling.

In speaking with parents and teachers regarding this issue, the following comments and suggestions were offered:

- Parents need to be more attuned to the educational process and how they can support their child.

- ✓ The back-to-school parent night is a great start, but it isn't enough. Prior to the start of the school year, teachers should reach out to all their students' parents by telephone. Before calling, teachers should know the background of each student, such as their academic strengths and weaknesses, outside interests, artistic or music ability, and overall educational experience. To parent(s), it shows the teacher is already interested and excited to meet the new students. This is a great opportunity for teachers to begin building a positive partnership with the parent(s) and including them in all aspects of their child's learning.

- Teachers need to see themselves as independent professional educators, rather than as employees dictated by bureaucracy.

  - ✓ The word "educator" is used as a noun. An educator leaves a permanent impression upon those who are taught. Professional educators are constantly raising the bar and setting new standards within their profession. They have a work ethic that doesn't quit, enough humility to know it isn't about them, a passion for teaching, a love of kids and subjects they teach, a willingness to change, an open-door policy, ability to ignore clock watchers and an understanding that being a great teacher requires constant reinventing and improving of oneself.

  - ✓ Professional educators are also known as "great teachers." Great teachers are in the talent-finding and talent-development business—a dyslexic student's dream teacher.

- No whining allowed. Parents don't like it when teachers complain about school issues, their jobs and how it affects their ability to teach. Teachers don't like it when parents complain, yet are never available to be part of the solution.

  - ✓ Never complain without having a possible solution in your back pocket. Parents and teachers must work together and come up with options that work best for the student. Think student first.

- Teachers believe that parents need to co-teach from home. Parents believe that teachers need to teach academics based on their résumés for employment.

    ✓ Teacher expectations of parents' co-teaching at home are not realistic. Parent(s) teach their children many things, but doing the educator's job is not one of them. That's why taxpayers pay educators to teach their children in academics.

    ✓ Parent expectations of teacher(s)' co-parenting at school are not realistic. Educator(s) teach their students many things, but expecting the teacher to stay after school while the student finishes homework is not one of them.

    ✓ Parent(s) and teacher(s) need to clarify their roles with one another and expect those involved to do their designated jobs.

- Teachers want parent participation in the classroom. Parents want to participate during academic time and not just when it involves fundraising, classroom parties or field day.

    ✓ At the beginning of the school year, teachers should write a letter to parents, asking for assistance in the classroom. The letter should define all areas of help needed throughout the school year, including academic support, in-class projects, group reading, and assistance in presenting a particular curriculum about which the parent may have special talent or knowledge. Teachers should then follow up with email communications with monthly classroom syllabus, events and special projects, and make it easy for parents to respond as to how they can help.

- Parents want video cameras in the classrooms to monitor teacher and student behavior. Teachers want professional autonomy.

    ✓ Teachers should have an open-door policy where parents are invited to visit the classroom any at any time. Parents can monitor teacher/student perceptions and gain insight to support their child.

- Parents want more positive (and less negative) feedback from teachers, including solutions and goals to help the student. Teachers want teacher-to-parent communications to be valued and responsive. Sometimes parent(s) feel the teacher doesn't like their child because the negative feedback outweighs the positive. Sometimes the teacher feels the parent(s) don't like them because they're dissatisfied with their child's academic progress. Both have valid concerns.

  ✓ The best way to deal with these concerns is to be honest and upfront as to why and how one feels. If teachers are overly negative, bringing it to their attention may be enough to change their perspective. If a parent seems distant, wishing for more open communication between them may invite collaboration.

- Neither wants to be told what to do.

  ✓ This is a sensitive one. Some teachers don't like parents telling them how or what works best in teaching their child. And some parents don't like being told by teacher(s) their child won't get into college unless their grades improve, and to consider alternative schooling. If this occurs, an independent educational mediator may be necessary.

- Both want a positive parent-teacher relationship that benefits the child/student.

  ✓ Thankfully, most parents and teachers have the same goal, but they disagree as to how to accomplish it. Both may show ignorance; that's okay, as long as they're willing to understand their differences and cooperate to the benefit of the student.

Jill age 8

"If there is something wrong, those
that have the ability to act, have
the responsibility to take action."

-Anonymous

CHAPTER 23

Ignoring the Signs

Parents Who Ignore the Signs

Parents sometimes fear that having a child labeled as learning disabled by the education world is more harmful than struggling privately with an undiagnosed learning disability. They worry that such a label will have a negative effect on the child's self-esteem.

Yet, when it comes to acknowledging that their child is struggling with a learning disability, some parents ignore the signs and convince themselves that nothing is wrong.

In one study, more than 50% of parents who noted that their child was exhibiting signs of a learning deficiency, waited a year or more before acknowledging that there might be a serious problem.

Other parents will disagree with the right path for their dyslexic child, citing as the reason immaturity, an expectation that the child will eventually outgrow it or a belief that the child just needs to work harder or needs more attention or more discipline.

Some parents will even go as far as hiding their child's learning disability symptoms by:

- Doing their child's homework.

- Showing them how to cheat on tests.

- Accusing the teacher of grading tests too hard.

- Refusing to acknowledge teacher concerns.

- Changing schools.

None of these tactics really work, except to delay the necessity for evaluating, diagnosing and treating the child's learning disability. Meanwhile, the dyslexic child continues to suffer and not receive the necessary academic support.

Teachers Who Ignore the Signs

Teachers are usually a child's first line of academic success. They encourage learning in a positive educational environment and never give up on their students.

Yet, when it comes to acknowledging that a student is struggling from a possible learning disability such as dyslexia, some teachers ignore the signs and resign themselves to thinking that the student is just a slow learner. In most cases, this is due to lack of teacher knowledge and training on dyslexia.

Sadly, some teachers will discourage parents from requesting an evaluation, suggesting that their children will be negatively labeled with a learning disability for the rest of their lives.

Other teachers fear that if they refer a student for evaluation for a possible learning disability, there will be consequences to themselves, such as:

- Having to attend numerous parent and special education meetings.

- Having to spend more focused time with the identified student and less time with other students.

- Being reprimanded by the principal or administration for recommending assessment of a student when the school is in a financial budget crisis.

- Being accused by the principal or superiors that they are not teaching properly and more effort on their part is all that is needed.

- The parents' being upset because the teacher is suggesting that their child may have a learning disability.

- Being told by the principal or administration that they have already met their quota for identifying and referring students for learning disabilities.

- Becoming frustrated when no action is taken after their referral for evaluation is made.

None of these concerns or excuses help the dyslexic student. A professional educator is required to pursue what is in the best interests of the student and not be influenced by fear or ignorance of others.

Allison age 11

"Education is learning what you
didn't know, you didn't know."

-Daniel J. Boorstin
American historian

CHAPTER 24

School/Teacher Delay Tactics and Excuses

The education world contains a lot of misinformation and inaccurate beliefs as to the required support of children with learning disabilities. Improperly trained educators are the main cause, although many inaccuracies and excuses include ignorance.

It's therefore no surprise that not all referrals for evaluation for a learning disability are openly welcomed by school administrators and/or teachers. Below are some of the delay tactics and excuses used to delay or deny evaluation:

- Schools don't diagnose dyslexia because they're not medical professionals.

- It's school policy not to evaluate students for a learning disability until the 2nd or 3rd grade.

- Signs of dyslexia are not identifiable until age seven or eight or older.

- The student is not mature enough for an evaluation.

- Evaluations are not allowed on students that are passing.

- The student is not far enough behind academically to qualify to receive an evaluation for a learning disability.

- The student's grades are fairly good and therefore does not qualify for an evaluation for a learning disability.

- Response to interventions must first be implemented before referral to receive evaluation for a learning disability.

- The teacher(s) believe the student is unmotivated or lazy and just needs to apply him/herself more. An evaluation for a learning disability will not solve the student's problem.

- The student doesn't need an evaluation. He/she just needs more support from the parent(s) or help from a tutor.

- The student has emotional issues, which are causing the academic problems. The school does not conduct evaluations for students with emotional issues.

- The student just needs medicine so that they can focus better on their schoolwork.

- The school does not provide evaluations for dyslexia or other processing issues.

- The school does not provide evaluations merely because the student has socialization problems.

- Teachers cannot provide educational support and/or accommodations unless the student is eligible for special-education support services.

- The school is not properly staffed or equipped to perform evaluations for learning disabilities.

- The school is low on funds and cannot afford anymore evaluations for learning disabilities.

- The school quota for evaluations has already been met this school year.

- It may be several weeks or months before the evaluation can be performed, and there are several students still waiting.

- Evaluations and IEPs (Individual Education Program) are a grueling process and may not result in eligibility for special education services.

- Children with dyslexia usually do not qualify for an evaluation or IEP.

- The student's teacher(s) must first agree that an evaluation is necessary.

- The student seems intelligent. Students with dyslexia are usually slow and cannot read.

- If the student has dyslexia, an evaluation will not make any difference because they will never learn to read well.

- Dyslexia is very rare and the school is not equipped or able to administer such an evaluation.

- The school only evaluates students for specific learning disabilities and cannot evaluate for dyslexia.

- A student who struggles with reading is just a slow learner, which is not a learning disability.

- The number of students needing evaluation is out of control. Parents are abusing requests for evaluations when it is not needed.

- Just because the student is being bullied by other students, doesn't mean they have a learning disability.

- Everyone is a little dyslexic—the student will grow out of it.

- Dyslexia is not that serious.

- Dyslexia is not life threatening.

George age 14

"A mother's love for her child is like nothing else in the world. It knows no aw, no pity, it dares all things and crushes down remorselessly all that stands in its path."

-Agatha Christie
American author

CHAPTER 25

Responding to Delay Tactics and Excuses

It is important that parent(s) feel empowered to respond to delay tactics and excuses that deny an evaluation for their child. The following suggested responses will encourage schools to do otherwise:

- Dyslexia is a term used to describe a reading disability. Using the term dyslexia is not a label problem, it's a "lack of understanding of what dyslexia is" problem.

- Although the school policy is to wait until the student reaches a certain age or grade before evaluating, this policy is not compliant with the law. The school's "waiting to fail" plan, requiring the student to first underperform academically, is not an acceptable method for determining when a student shall be evaluated for a potential learning disability.

- According to the medical and scientific community, children as young as five years old are accurately evaluated and diagnosed with learning disabilities such as dyslexia.

- In order to complete an evaluation, the school must use multiple methods and strategies when determining special education eligibility, including grades, test scores, student work samples, teacher input and parent input, as well as evaluations and assessments from a school psychologist or educational therapist, including private evaluation by a clinical psychologist, pediatric neuropsychologist or other professional specializing in educational learning disabilities.

- Although the school believes the student's grades are good enough, it doesn't mean they cannot be evaluated. Nowhere in the law does it state that having fairly good grades denies a student for evaluation or eligibility for special education and/ or support services.

- The law does not prohibit schools from evaluating a student for a learning disability while the student simultaneously receives academic interventions. A response to intervention program cannot be used as an excuse or reason for delaying evaluation.

- Although feedback from the teacher(s) is important, the parent(s) may not believe their child is unmotivated or lazy but instead is struggling academically and is in need of evaluation for a possible learning disability.

- A student's emotional and social well being is just as important, and access to the curriculum means more than just academics.

- The law mandates that schools receiving government funds must locate, identify and refer for evaluation, all school-aged children who are in need of special education and related services, with or without a referral from the parents or guardians. Therefore, a referral from parents requires compliance with the law.

- No law prohibits schools from evaluating or providing special education services based on quotas or the number of students eligible.

- Schools that deny evaluations or special education services based on school funding are in violation of the law.

- The law provides that evaluations, assessments and special education services be provided within specific timeframes and not at school discretion.

- Specific tests and protocols are administered when evaluating students with possible learning disabilities. Therefore, the opinions or views of others, as to the dynamics, symptoms, diagnosis or outcomes, cannot be decided by non-qualified entities or persons.

- Students with dyslexia are just as intelligent as non-dyslexic students. Dyslexic students have specific learning preferences, just as non-dyslexics have their specific learning preferences.

- The growing number of students needing evaluation for a learning disability has nothing to do with parent excuses and everything to do with public education and awareness. Education and public awareness is paramount if parents want to advocate for their children.

- For parents, a child with a learning disability is very serious, especially if surrounded by educators and/or administrators who are ignorant of dyslexia and not equipped to help them.

Harrison age 8

"Nothing great is ever achieved by doing things the way they have always been done."

-Anonymous

CHAPTER 26

Parent Delay Tactics and Excuses

Some parents deny or reject suggestions that their child be evaluated for a possible learning disability. They may react defensively, believing their child is being negatively targeted or labeled as learning disabled without cause. Anger, blaming others and guilt can take center stage, leaving the child stuck in the middle.

Dyslexic children are not learning disabled when they receive appropriate support and educational therapies.

The following delay tactics and excuses by parents are not valid reasons for denying an evaluation:

- The student is not doing well in school because the teacher and student are not a good match and don't work well together.

- As long as the school passes the student, that's good enough.

- The student doesn't need an Individualized Education Program. The parent(s) claim they have dyslexia, never had an IEP and turned out all right.

- Parents believe that whatever it is, their child will grow out of it.

- Parents claim they cannot attend evaluation and IEP meetings because they work and have other priorities.

- Parents do not want their child labeled with a learning disability because it will prevent them from getting into a good college/ university or getting a good job.

- Parents do not want their child placed in any special educational support classes because other students will make fun of the student's lack of intelligence.

- Parents believe the school is taking retribution by claiming their child may have a learning disability.

- Parents don't know who to believe. The teacher feels the student may have a learning disability, but the principal does not agree.

- Parents claim their other children don't have any problems. Their black-sheep child is the runt of the litter and is just slow.

- Parents believe their child is unmotivated and lazy and will suffer the consequences of not working hard. It's the child's problem, not theirs.

- The student is in high school and failing every subject. There is no hope. The student's path in life has already been shaped and is set in stone.

- The student has been in and out of juvenile detention facilities and nothing has changed.

- Parents do not have the energy to deal with their child's academic problems anymore. They're exhausted.

- Parents believe that their tax dollars are not being spent wisely on their child, which is the reason the child is not doing well.

- Parents resent re-teaching or tutoring their child outside of school and are not willing to do anything more.

- Parents believe that dyslexia is not that serious and certainly is not life threatening.

"There are two primary choices in life: to accept conditions as they exist, or accept the responsibility for changing them."

-Denis Waitley, American author

Monique age 13

"Never doubt that a small group of thoughtful,
committed citizens can change the world.
Indeed, it is the only thing that ever has."

-Margaret Mead
Cultural anthropologist

CHAPTER 27

The Power of Parents

The parent and child bond is incredibly strong. Parents' leaving their children for the first time with a pre-school/childcare provider can be a momentous event. Separation anxiety kicks in, and parents have a difficult time leaving the classroom, never mind the campus. Love notes to their child, snacks and written instructions to the teacher, are carefully itemized and organized, depending on nap time and play time.

At this age, teachers/caregivers dutifully follow what parents instruct, almost without question. After all, parents know their children best, and those caring for them make every effort to fulfill the parents' requests.

Parent input and concerns however, seem to change when their child begins elementary school. The "power baton" gets passed on, leaving parents feeling compelled to depend on school administrators and teachers for knowing what is best for their child academically. For parents, such submission is a mistake, when dependency and learned helplessness replace advocacy. In other words, parents become more reliant and dependent on school-system decisions, believing that schools and teachers have all the required training and knowledge they lack. They want to trust their child's school and teachers to do what is in the best interest of every child, no matter what. This is all too true when parents give entire decision-making power over to outsiders who barely know their child.

Sadly, most teachers are ill-equipped to teach children with dyslexia and openly admit to their lack of knowledge.

So what are parents to do? The answer is simple. Learn. Learn everything there is to know about their child's learning difficulties. Parents should never exclusively rely on school administrators, teachers, school psychologists, etc., as the ultimate academic authority.

Being a parent leader or advocate does not require any special talents or academic credentials, except a willingness to seek out information, as well as a driving passion to help their child, regardless of the obstacles.

Thanks to technology, the Internet, and books on dyslexia, parents can stay informed, gather resources, engage and exchange ideas and influence positive change, simply by becoming more knowledgeable in the academic needs of their child.

Knowledge equals empowerment.

"There are only two ways to
live your life. One is as though
nothing is a miracle. The other is
as though everything is a miracle."

-Albert Einstein, Physicist

Jacob age 10

"Tell me and I'll forget.
Show me and I may remember.
Involve me and I'll understand."

-Proverb

CHAPTER 28

Brain-Friendly Classrooms and Schools

Picture it… the teacher happily greets students in the morning, excited to start the day. The classroom is comfortable, reflecting student work, colorful artwork, positive messages, engaging curriculum, and welcoming ways to learn. Brain-friendly classrooms incorporate many of these qualities, because they know:

We learn five percent from a lecture, ten percent of what we read, twenty percent of what we hear, thirty percent of what we see, fifty percent of what we both see and hear, seventy percent of discussed with others, eighty percent of what we experience personally, and ninety five percent of what we just learned and immediately use or apply.

—Eldon Ekwall

Brain-friendly classrooms and schools are "emotionally engaging." Students learn best when their environment has certain elements that embody safety, movement, novelty, preview, processing time, interest level, engagement, organized spacing, music and positive feedback. These elements are necessary in setting the tone for a successful emotional stage within the classroom and campus climate.

Brain-friendly classrooms and schools provide:

- Safety—physically and emotionally safe environments in the classroom, on the playground, on the school bus and during off campus field trips.

- Movement—students kinesthetically respond to project classwork with movement and collaboration with other students. Students move freely within the classroom when collaborating and exploring new ideas and knowledge with classmates, which teaches problem-solving skills and natural respect among peers.

- Novelty—students like their teacher(s), enjoy their out of the box techniques for learning and gravitate to unexpected surprises without hesitation. Novelty includes relevance, curiosity, emotion, stories, questions, problems, visual output, drama, antidotes, guessing games, humor and quotations.

- Preview—curiosity and intrigue encourage surprising displays of what is to come—tomorrow, next week or next semester.

- Processing time—students have adequate time to process information. This involves time given to explore new knowledge. Presentation of new information is engaging and patient and provides ample time for processing and learning.

- Teacher engagement—not "teaching to the bell" or repeating the same teaching style every day as the norm. Instead, teacher presents information in 15-minute increments, followed by discussion and settling time (pair time, quiet music or quiet-choice time).

- Interest Level—zoned out, dozed out students do not exist in brain-friendly classrooms. Teachers encourage students with choices in ways to learn and express themselves. Student learning styles are focused on positive outcomes.

- Student Engagement—an enriched environment with lots of hands on activities, real world applications and engaging resource materials, including high-interest books, technology, audio and visual presentations and former student work samples.

- Organized spacing—backpacks and lunch boxes are stowed on shelving and/or hooks, school supplies are organized and students have a clear, unobstructed view of the teacher and learning board.

- Music—nothing lightens the mood and elevates one's consciousness more than music. Brain-friendly classrooms spontaneously incorporate music into the curriculum. Learning is unexpectedly fun—on purpose.

- Positive feedback—teacher(s) provide continuous daily feedback and assess student learning in a variety of ways (a body of work) beyond testing.

Brain-friendly classrooms improve student memory, energize learning, and illuminate reasoning and problem solving. Teachers who have time to teach only content, should get a shovel and cover up that content with dirt because most of their students' potential will be left uncovered.

Forrest age 14

"I've come to the frightening conclusion, that I am the decisive element in the classroom. My personal approach creates a climate. My daily mood makes the weather. As a teacher, I possess tremendous power to make a child's life miserable or joyous. I can be the tool of torture or an instrument of inspiration. I can humiliate or humor, hurt or heal. In all situations, it is my responses that decides whether a crisis will be escalated or de-escalated and a child humanized or de-humanized."

-Haim Ginott, Psychologist and Educator

CHAPTER 29

Dyslexia-Friendly Classroom

One of the basic principles of creating a dyslexia-friendly classroom is the expectation that teacher(s) take immediate action when faced with students who have specific learning needs, rather than waiting until an evaluation determines approval or denial for special educational services.

In dyslexia-friendly schools, teachers become empowered with training and knowledge. They identify learning differences, take front line action and apply "student first" needs without hesitation.

With these principles in mind, the following are examples of what a dyslexia-friendly teacher/classroom looks like:

- Teacher's handwriting is in a clear, readable format, avoiding print/writing combinations, scribbling, abbreviated words and incomplete sentences.

- Assignment handouts, worksheets and test sheets are in a dyslexia-friendly font (such as Avenir), text size at 12 to 13 points (depending on font used) and with generous line spacing. Less information on each page, with a less-cluttered text, is crucial. The layout and presentation of worksheets are just as important as their content and the tasks they describe.

- Teachers use clearly spoken instructions (even toned, and slower paced, which is easily repeated or paused). Simplified sentences are more effective. Why use 30 words when 10 will do?

- Daily assignments are clearly posted on the board at the beginning of class, in large enough lettering. Teachers are aware of their penmanship and readability. Copies or computer printouts of daily assignments are also provided.

- There is less teacher lecturing, and there are more kinesthetic teaching applications.

- Vocabulary or high-frequency words are clearly posted on the board. A copy or computer printout of these words is given to the dyslexic student.

- A "buddy support system" is in place for all students.

- Dyslexic students are placed in the front of the class with an unobstructed view of the board and teacher during instruction.

- Teacher(s) communicate "high expectations" (can do culture) with all students, including those students with dyslexia.

- Teachers break down instructions into small, logical chunks and communicate the order of completion.

- The teacher checks in often during classwork, ensuring that the dyslexic student is understanding and completing the assignment.

- Classrooms provide portable writing aides/laptops, text to speech options, etc., for reading support.

- Teacher(s) apply the dyslexic student's Individualized Education Program (IEP) and/or support, with knowledge and understanding.

- All teachers and administrators apply "whole school" best practices for students with dyslexia.

"The mediocre teacher tells. The good teacher explains. The superior teacher demonstrates. The great teacher inspires."

- Ritu Ghatourey, Indian inspirational author

Samantha age 10

"To successfully manage the inclusive
classroom, teachers should re-examine
the notion of what is "fair. Fair does
not mean that every pupil gets the
same treatment, but that every
pupil gets what he or she needs".

-Anonymous

CHAPTER 30

The Student's Perspective: Dyslexia-Friendly Teacher

Children with dyslexia share a natural ability to spot a dyslexia-friendly teacher and how their understanding and knowledge translate into academic success. Dyslexic students describe their teacher(s) as, "My teacher gets it—my teacher gets me!"

Teacher(s) that "get it" reflect incredible confidence in their abilities to help dyslexic students.

Consistent attributes that describe a dyslexia-friendly teacher include the following:

- Provides clear, easy to understand instructions.

- Provides written instructions that are clearly printed on the board at the beginning of class.

- Allows enough time for the student to correctly write instructions, followed by teacher confirmation that instructions are correct.

- Is prepared to repeat using a different explanation of the instructions until they are clearly understood by the student.

- Understands that dyslexic students may need time to process and understand instructions and patiently allows time for their response.

- Proactively offers help (recognizing that dyslexic students may feel intimidated or embarrassed to ask on their own).

- Is patient and understanding.

- Is approachable and answers questions freely.

- Never forces the dyslexic student to read aloud in class.

- Is creative and makes lessons fun and practical.

- Is comfortable asking questions to better understand student needs.

- Never shames the dyslexic student, privately or publicly.

- Offers one-to-one support without the need for special education eligibility.

- Provides teacher and/or peer notes.

- Accepts oral testing when requested.

- Allows more time on assignments and tests.

- Accepts dyslexia as a learning disability and not a crutch that is fixable.

- Does not resent the dyslexic student for receiving educational support.

- Offers organizational tips in helpful ways.

- Encourages the dyslexic student and rewards good attempts.

- Provides a calm and emotionally safe classroom environment.

- Likes the dyslexic student and shows genuine interest in engaging them.

- Respects the dyslexic student's anonymity of their learning difference and does not share or discuss these differences with other students.

- Has high expectations for dyslexic students, irrespective of their learning preference.

- Smiles when the dyslexic student has questions or needs clarification.

"The test for a good teacher is not how many questions he can ask his pupils that they will answer readily, but how many questions he inspires them to ask him which he finds it hard to answer."

- Alice Wellington Rollins,
(1847-1897), Author

Sydney age 13

"There is nothing more unfair than the equal treatment of unequal people."

-Thomas Jefferson
3rd President of the United States

CHAPTER 31

Fairness

Some teachers personally struggle with what fairness in education means when it involves children with learning disabilities. That struggle usually stems from a lack of knowledge and training in these areas.

However, teachers who receive professional training on dyslexia typically do not struggle with the same emotional fairness conflicts that are seen in untrained teachers. Properly trained educators concur on the following:

- Teachers with proper training understand "fairness" means every student gets what he or she needs. A level playing field is likened to accepting an innocent newborn—a new and different family member—into your inner circle.

- Trained teachers know that fairness has nothing to do with other students. Nor does fairness mean all students should be treated the same. Fairness in teaching dyslexic students simply means they receive what they need to succeed academically. To be fair, teachers must teach in the way their students learn.

- Fairness develops by what one sees. Children watch visual signals and naturally emulate them, even when what they see is morally wrong. It is extremely important for teachers to know what strategies encourage fairness in their curriculum and differentiated instruction, without doubt and hesitation. If a teacher is not convinced all students should be treated fairly by getting what they need, then resentment will rear its ugly head and discrimination will take center stage.

- Educators who believe fairness requires only ensuring that students with learning disabilities "fit in" and "not stick out" show a lack of professional training. This translates into not wanting to teach them differently, which is unfair and discriminatory.

- Trained educators know that the fairness doctrine covers 95% of a student's time in the classroom, and not just during special education services.

- Special education services represent a small adjunct to student support. The classroom teacher is responsible for implementing the majority of that support.

- One size fits all education is not realistic. Educators who feel that one size fits all teaching is fair should probably find another line of work.

CHAPTER 32

Misdiagnosed with "Other Health Impairment"

As previously discussed, it is not uncommon for children with dyslexia to be diagnosed with something other than dyslexia, such as ADD or ADHD.

Unfortunately, an epidemic exists among school-aged children on medication. And one in five college students abuse prescription stimulants typically prescribed for attention-deficit/hyperactivity disorder (ADHD).

Some teachers associate a struggling student with ADD/ADHD, even when the symptoms describe dyslexia. This happens when teachers lack education on dyslexia and default to believing the student needs to be medicated, and encourage parents to consult with their child's doctor.

There is no pill for children with dyslexia. Trying to medicate them is not a substitute for academic support. It is crucial that parents be educated and informed in knowing the differences between dyslexia and other health impairments so that their children receive the correct support.

For comparison, parents may wish to use the following symptoms list for ADD/ADHD, as a guide and further discussion with their child's doctor:

ADD/ADHD symptoms include:

An inability to stay focused for a period of time. (distracted, inattentive and uninterested)

- Pays poor attention to detail.

- Has trouble listening when others are talking.

- Daydreams excessively; seems preoccupied.

- Is tired, sluggish or slow moving.

- Appears apathetic or unmotivated; bored.

- Has difficulty sustaining attention span for most tasks.

- A tendency to act without thinking (impulsivity).

  - Engages in dangerous behavior (for example, running into the street without looking).

  - Is unable to wait for his/her turn.

  - Blurts inappropriate comments.

  - When upset, hits another child.

- An inability to sit still and focus (hyperactivity).

  - Talks excessively and/or interrupts.

  - Engages in excessive or constant activity, movement and motion.

  - Is constantly on the move, running, jumping or screaming.

  - Is aggressive and has difficulties controlling behavior.

Important Notes:

- It is against the law for a teacher, principal, special education specialist or other school administrator to require medication intervention as a condition for a student to receive academic support.

- If a student is taking medication and shows no further signs of difficulty at school, he or she may no longer be eligible for academic support. In other words, if the school deems the student's disability no longer affects learning, educational support services may no longer be necessary.

"We must make the choices that enable us to fulfill the deepest capacities of our real selves".

– Thomas Merton (1915-1968),
American writer and poet

CHAPTER 33

Educational Drugs

In the past decade, the use of medically prescribed drugs by school-age children has more than tripled. These drugs, also known as educational drugs, prescribe medication, suggesting help with focus on their school work.

Some teachers recommend to parents that their child be medicated because they believe the student's classroom performance will improve. And although teachers are not doctors, parents dutifully listen and believe their recommendations, irrespective of whether the student has an IEP (Individualized Education Program) that teacher(s) and school must follow.

An IEP never recommends that the student needs medication to help them focus. Instead, an IEP provides educational therapies that will help the student succeed in school. Why then do some teachers offer medical advice to medicate a student? Is it because they believe these drugs are harmless and would benefit the student, or because it helps the teacher teach the student?

For the record, there is no pill for dyslexia. There is no pill that will help improve their short-term working memory—no pill to improve their ability to remember or process information longer—no pill that makes them learn like other students—and no pill to stop them from learning the way they need to.

Children with dyslexia are sometimes misdiagnosed and prescribed educational drugs. These drugs alter the way the brain processes information, which can lead to emotional and physical addiction to the drug(s) prescribed.

Children with dyslexia often struggle with anxiety and stress. If medicated with educational drugs, they're often denied the opportunity to learn appropriate coping skills that will sustain them through life.

The best course of action in helping children with dyslexia includes specifically designed educational therapies that support learning.

Sarah age 16

"My best childhood memory was falling asleep on the couch and waking up in bed thinking…. Wow, I can teleport."

-Anonymous

CHAPTER 34

Short-Term and Long-Term Memory

Imagine not having the daily ability to remember simple instructions in completing tasks, the order of those tasks or if the tasks have been done correctly. Most people would become quickly frustrated and take steps to correct their misdirection.

Dyslexic children, however, have problems remembering information, whether simple or complex—their daily norm.

School-aged children learn and process a great deal of daily new information. An efficient memory is critical to a child's social and academic development and success. Dyslexic children with memory deficits are at an unfortunate disadvantage and struggle with remembering directions, solving problems and recalling information. Memory deficits negatively affect the dyslexic child's school experience and home environment, as well as dramatically impact their overall well-being.

Unfortunately, teachers and/or parents may misinterpret signs of memory deficits and assume the child is purposely ignoring directions or is simply a slow learner. Without an appropriate psycho-educational evaluation to define these deficits, misconceptions by adult authority figures can lead to poor academic performance, including behavior issues and a lifetime of failure for the dyslexic child.

In order to help dyslexic students with educational support, it is important to understand the different types of memory deficits and their symptoms. Children with dyslexia live with memory deficits that cannot be corrected. They are at a serious disadvantage, which affects every aspect of their everyday lives, including their ability to succeed academically.

Short-Term Working Memory

Dyslexic children with short-term memory deficits experience difficulty holding information for immediate processing. Short-term working memory is the brain's "sticky-note taker," which is used for short-term "storage" of information received visually, spatially and verbally. Working memory helps keep more things in mind while approaching a task.

With verbal (auditory) working memory deficit, pieces of information often evade ones grasp, leaving very little to act upon to complete the task. Due to this weakness, the dyslexic student is not able to effectively follow a multi-step set of oral instructions. If short-term memory is overloaded, parts of what is supposed to be remembered will be lost and the reading process will fail.

Visual (spatial) working memory involves envisioning something, to keep it in the "mind's eye," such as to remember patterns, images and sequences of events (as in mathematical equations). If not identified, deficits in visual working memory are ripe for misunderstanding and accusation of not paying attention.

For the dyslexic student, having a weak working memory is mentally exhausting in a learning environment. Combine these challenges with high anxiety, which also puts demands on working memory, and the learning process becomes all the more painful.

Memory deficit symptoms include:

- Not remembering what they see, hear or present.

- Often forgetting pronunciation of commonly used words.

- Weak spelling.

- Difficulty remembering the order of directions/instructions.

- Weak sight words and vocabulary.

- Being slow to develop reading skills.

- Difficulty memorizing facts, speeches and rhymes.

- Use of correct nouns only rarely, instead referring to "that thing" or "you know."

- Weak expressive and receptive language.

- Frequent repetition of the same errors and mistakes.

- Often appearing forgetful.

- Abandonment of activities before completing them.

- Often seeming to daydream.

- Forgetting how to continue an activity to end, even though the teacher has explained the steps.

- Confusing instructions with current ones.

- Difficulty copying instructions within the time provided.

- Receiving poor grades on tests requiring memorization of facts or figures or the writing of long essays.

- Often unable to recall or remember important details just read in a passage or chapter in a book.

- Difficulty remembering lists of things over a period of time.

Short-Term Memory Teaching Strategies

Dyslexic are at a tremendous disadvantage with short-term working memory issues. Accommodations and appropriate teaching strategies in this area are critical to their academic success.

Dyslexic students that do not receive the proper teaching strategies and/or accommodations, will continue to struggle academically.

The following teaching strategies are recommended:

- Teach "sight" vocabulary/learning with pictures/diagrams using two second memory game responses.

- Use a "top-down" approach to instruction. Top-down teaching style focuses on providing students with the "big picture" without explaining the details. Students instead plunge into the visual completion and then gradually learn the building blocks that make up the result.

- Break instructions into parts, presenting only one or two parts at a time, verifying understanding before moving on.

- Teach information in easily recognized groups or families to help memory.

- When teaching, offer a written or pictorial model the student can refer to.

- Write key terms on the board so that the student can readily refer to them.

- Consider presenting sequential information in the form of a song or rhyme.

- Instruct all students to "immediately write down the following" information as stated by the teacher (such as key concepts and/or vocabulary).

- During oral instruction or lectures, move slowly, repeat key information often and write key words and concepts on the board.

- During a lecture, offer a formatted, written fill-in-the-blank script for the student to write in key words/concepts.

- Provide extra time for copying information or provide information already in copied form.

- Teach using a multi-sensory (simultaneously engaging all senses – visual, auditory, tactile and kinesthetic) approach, so that students use as many channels as possible to absorb and store information.

- Teach letter sounds and spelling with "look, say, trace, cover, write and check, of letters and words.

Jose' age 12

"Living in dreams of yesterday,
we find ourselves still dreaming
of impossible future conquests."

-Charles Lindbergh
American aviator
1902-1974

Long-Term Memory

Although it is well documented that differences in non-verbal long-term memory tasks are good predictors of reading difficulties in dyslexics, rarely is long-term memory testing included with an educational evaluation.

Long-term memory testing involves three parts. The first part is "episodic memory," which refers to our recall of personal experiences from our past, such as details from our early childhood, details of a movie we saw last week or what we ate for breakfast. This aspect of memory organizes information around "episodes" in our lives. The second part is "semantic memory," which refers to "meaningful," easily related events that associate current with past experiences. It is through these associative connections that we are able to retrieve, accept and store information in the future. The third part is "procedural memory," which refers to the ability to remember and perform tasks; when we retrieve information from procedural memory, we retrieve one step, which triggers the next step, and the next, etc. These three parts work together and are a component of an inclusive and extensive education evaluation.

Two major challenges are related to the use of long-term memory. The first challenge is to transfer information accurately to long-term memory. (Transferring information from working memory to long-term memory is called encoding.) The second challenge is to retrieve the information accurately. Children with dyslexia have difficulty moving and/or retrieving information to and from long-term memory.

The key ingredient that nurtures long-term storage is "meaningfulness," and it refers to information already stored in our long-term memory. Meaningfulness relates to the establishing of connections between new and old information that is already stored. As an example, ten pieces of information in long-term memory related to a particular topic have a better chance of being more meaningful than only one related piece of information stored in memory.

A student with a richer background or experience trumps an equally intelligent student with no background knowledge related to the topic. One way to create meaningfulness is to connect, or associate, the new material being learned, to current events, popular movies, songs, etc. Students can then elaborate on material by connecting it to material already in their own minds.

Techniques that enable students to connect prior information and experiences to existing information and experiences are likely to increase meaningfulness and the ease with which information is later recalled from long-term memory. Enabling students to make information more meaningful requires a more active approach to teaching new knowledge.

Long-Term Memory Teaching Strategies

As with short-term memory deficits, long-term memory deficits also require accommodations with teaching strategies during academic learning.

The following teaching strategies are recommended:

- Help relate relationships between new information and other information that is already in long-term memory.

- Suggest differences between new information and other information that is already in long-term memory.

- Treat information actively, not passively. Provide information in meaningful ways, having the student diagram it, outline it or ask questions about it.

- Help students visualize and form mental images that associate a term or event to be recalled.

- Encourage students to express their reasoning of new information within an open, friendly classroom discussion, allowing sufficient time to formulate responses.

- Assist students with decoding of words by saying the sounds and then pausing to allowing time to respond.

- Discuss the meaning of a story read by sharing what the teacher feels and understands before asking students to respond.

- Encourage sharing of student life experiences that may relate to new information learned.

- While reading a passage, actively solicit answers to questions that confirm understanding.

- Use "episodic cues" to recall information, through smell, objects, colors, feelings, etc.

- Express vocabulary words within sentences and stories.

- Imagine details and feelings. Have students imagine themselves in the scene, viewing things as if they are actually there.

- Have students create "memory books" that use pictures, family photos, magazine clip art/pictures, etc. to tell a story.

"Let your life lightly dance on the edges of time, like dew on the tip of a leaf."

-Rabindranath Tagore (1861 - 1941),
Writer and painter. Nobel
Prize in Literature in 1913

Sophie age 9

"Some people feel the rain,
while others just get wet."

-Bob Marley
Jamaican reggae singer/musician
1945-1981

CHAPTER 35

Accessibility in Education with Accommodations

The term "accessibility" in education is misunderstood. Having accessibility to public education does not mean simply having access to textbooks, teachers and classrooms. It means having textbooks with readability, teachers with training on teaching to children with learning disabilities and classrooms that are friendly to the accessible environment.

For example, children with dyslexia benefit from receiving educational accessibility, such as textbooks, assignments and tests with readability and text size at 12 points or higher (depending on the font), wider spacing between sentences, and less information on the page. If textbooks, assignments or tests lack readability, have text size below 12 points, with standard spacing between sentences and more information on the page, then the textbooks, assignments and tests are "not accessible" to the dyslexic student.

Another example of accessibility is when a teacher slows down the pace of speaking and allows more time for responses to questions. If the teacher speaks to the student at a pace that the dyslexic student finds difficult to process and the student does not have enough time to respond, then the teacher's speaking pace and time spent awaiting a student's response are "not accessible" to the dyslexic student.

Accessibility in education means that school-aged children with specific learning disabilities receive educational accommodations that meet learning needs. It is therefore extremely important that children with dyslexia receive accessibility to education that benefits and supports their learning experience.

Laws define supplementary aids and services as aids, services and other supports that are provided in regular education classes, and include (but are not limited to):

- A structured learning environment.

- Repeating and simplifying instructions with regards to in-class and homework assignments.

- Supplementing verbal instructions with visual instructions.

- Using behavioral management techniques.

- Adjusting class schedules.

- Modifying test delivery.

- Use of recording devices, computer aided instruction and other audio visual equipment.

- Modified textbooks or workbooks.

- Tailoring homework assignments.

- Use of one-on-one tutorials, classroom aides and note takers.

- Involvement of a services coordinator to oversee implementation of accommodations and services.

The next several pages describe the types of accommodations and services that match the accessibility to education needed for children with dyslexia.

Harry age 11

"In the book of life, the
answers aren't in the back."

-Charlie Brown,
as written by Charles Schultz

Reading

Everyday learning occurs in many ways: auditory, visual and kinesthetic. However, learning by reading (by a large majority) has taken center stage as the main instrument used for acquiring new knowledge. This means that if one's learning style requires a more visual or kinesthetic approach, the student's education is not accessible. Their learning ability is at a disadvantage and their learning difference becomes even more accentuated.

For children with dyslexia, an overemphasis on reading, without including a knowledgeable balance of other learning senses and abilities, can negatively affect their overall learning experience. Over strenuous or repetitious reading demands do not improve the reading ability of the dyslexic student and never will. Children with dyslexia naturally prefer to receive, process and present information in the way that makes sense to them.

Most children with dyslexia are right-brain dominant. Because of this they see in pictures, not in words. For example, in the sentence, "The red wagon is on the lawn," non-dyslexics see the words, red, wagon and lawn. Dyslexics see a picture of a red wagon on a lawn, but not the words.

Children with dyslexia think faster than they read—so putting them in low ability groups and measuring them solely on reading ability wrongly labels them as failures or as slow, which impacts their self-esteem. Insisting on more reading does not work. What does work is for teachers to teach differently. The good news is that what works for dyslexics in the classroom can work well for all students.

Dyslexic children have difficulties with word recognition, decoding, spelling and comprehension (working memory deficits). Difficulties include:

- Naming, sequencing and writing the alphabet.

- Reading words that cannot be translated into mental pictures (such as and, a, and the).

- Seeing non-image words, such as at, after or last.

- Misreading words that are visually similar, such as was/saw, speak/break.

- Omitting connecting words, such as at, where, who, over, or under.

- Misreading multi-syllable words.

- Understanding complex test questions.

- Understanding "double negative" words in sentences.

- Reading aloud with repeated mistakes and pauses.

- Retelling the sequence of events in a story.

- Memorizing non-phonetic words.

- Sequencing letters to form a word.

- Reading numbers and mathematical symbols.

- Organizing what to say and unable to think of the word needed.

- Finding a word in the dictionary.

- Naming the days of the week and months of the year.

- Understanding inferences, jokes or sarcasm.

Children with dyslexia need the following accessible accommodations. Teachers should:

- Rely less on textbooks and more on activities that make reading and reading-by-learning assignments more interesting and relevant.

- Spend more time on building background for reading selections and creating mental images regarding the text.

- Offer to read written material aloud to the entire class.

- Read aloud material that is written on the board.

- Review or preview relevant material to be presented at the beginning and end of class.

- Make a list of required readings available early and arrange to obtain text/books on CD/tape/e-books or audio books for students with dyslexia.

- Accept family reading (between student and family member) as "minutes read per day" reading credit.

- Implement "reading on the road" during field trip events, whereby students identify "road signage" for group points and prizes.

- Use fun visuals and simulations when introducing new reading material. Dyslexics are "picture thinkers" and need both visual and auditory senses stimulated when reading.

- Provide advance notice to the student of any oral class reading, including the passage or paragraph.

- Promote reading for a range of purposes. Let students choose their own reading material (comics, funnies, magazine, newspaper, short stories, etc.) when the activity is about "reading for pleasure."

- Set an appropriate tone in the classroom. All students should feel comfortable and safe from ridicule, teasing, chuckling or laughter during oral reading.

- Encourage and compliment oral reading effort with an abundance of praise.

- Include "I spy" reading for chapter books with a "word bank" of clues necessary to complete the book assignment.

- Accept that not all learning is earned by reading text written by others.

- Provide partial outlines of books/chapter books.

- Provide in advance, a word bank of new words with definitions, from the book to be read.

- Have students create a storyboard that illustrates the sequence of main events in a story.

- Schedule storytelling sessions where the dyslexic student can retell a story recently read.

- Schedule play acting sessions where students can role play different characters in a story.

- Have the dyslexic student create a "word bank dictionary" of new or "hard to read" sight vocabulary words, which they can refer to just like a dictionary.

- Play board games that provide practice in reading comprehension or vocabulary words.

- Schedule computer game time that focuses on practicing sight vocabulary words.

- Be patient with their responses. Children with dyslexia can be highly articulate but often have to search for words, which gives the impression that they are unsure of what they are trying to say.

Reading Fluency

Reading fluency involves reading text smoothly and effortlessly, with expression and at an appropriate speed.

Children with dyslexia have limited fluency, read less text and are less likely to remember what they've just read. A lack of fluency results in slow processing speed.

The following are appropriate accessible accommodations to help improve fluency:

- Introduce dyslexic students to "Spritz" reading. Spritz reading (a computer software program) is reading text "one word at a time," with the ability to control reading speed as desired. Spritz reading aids in improving readability of text and comprehension.

- Introduce the entire class to read aloud "choral reading," which helps practicing phrasing and intonation. Choral reading should be done with a large copy of the text.

- Provide opportunities for students to listen to recordings of books while reading along aloud, but softly.

- Provide opportunities for students to listen to recordings of books while reading along.

- Choose a text between 50 and 100 words in length and play a "time" reading game.

- Choose a list of 30 to 40 high frequency words and play a 1 minute word reading game.

The best approach to improving a dyslexic's reading is not to "read like a non-dyslexic does," but to find a way of extracting information from text (written words) that work more effectively for the student who processes information differently from other readers.

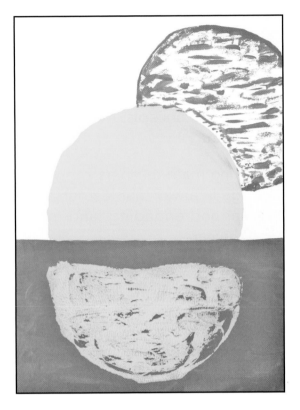

Jason age 14

"The words of language as they are written or spoken, don't play any role in my mechanism of thought."

-Albert Einstein
Scientist and inventor

Mathematics

Contrary to popular belief, learning mathematics is really creative and fun. Quite often, what ruins the experience is boring, repetitious instruction, copious amounts of note taking, rigid one way problem solving strategies, and awkwardly structured lecturing of mathematical concepts. It's no wonder why students disengage and zone out.

Out-of-the-box thinking math teachers know the difference and share their knowledge in a way that learners understand. These teachers are popular and engaging, and most students (and parents) know who they are.

The focus of some math teachers is more "black and white" and "the goal is the answer." For others, "the sky's the limit," and "there may be no answer, one answer, or many answers."

Teachers who are more left-brain dominant can have difficulties working with right-brain dominant students. Most children with dyslexia are right-brain dominant and have difficulties learning from left-brain, lecture-type teaching. Teachers whose style is predominately verbal will be a disadvantage to predominately visual learners because their cognitive styles are different. Mathematical difficulties for dyslexics include:

- Confusion with calculation signs, basic operations and facts.

- Trouble organizing problems on the page and keeping numbers lined up.

- Missing steps on multi-step calculations, such as long division, which is due to short-term memory deficits.

- Being unable to remember the order of mathematical operations, including recalling math rules, formulas and sequences.

- Difficulty copying from the board, which creates a disorganized layout of written work.

- Directional confusion—confused by inconsistent starting points for solving math problems (left/right, before/after).

Children with dyslexia prefer hands on, kinesthetic approaches to learning and teachings that transfer learning to real life, problem solving situations. Accessible accommodation in math for students with dyslexia is necessary and fair. Here are some examples:

- Allow students to draw illustrations or build models to explain, clarify and simplify math problems.

- Provide a range of real world connections as examples because students relate better to everyday events.

- Allow students to use math charts, such as "Flipper" charts. Flippers are simple, quick reference card charts, attached to each other, that follow the rules and sequences of math learning.

- Teach students to use a calculator and all of its functions. Learning how to apply calculator functions is a valuable tool students can learn at any age.

- Allow students to explore different strategies for getting the same answer. Students should feel encouraged to investigate different strategies without criticism.

- Allow students to know the answer and work backwards through to the question.

- Use a variety of materials (blocks, sticks, money, etc.) when teaching measurements, using hands on applications for student learning.

- Suggest "visual thinking" methods when teaching by association for math solutions.

- Provide cross-age peer tutoring, with a student in a higher grade functioning as the tutor. Cross-age peer tutoring is more beneficial for students with dyslexia, than within class peer-assisted tutoring.

- Good questions have more than one correct mathematical answer. Allow students to explore all possible answers and methods.

- On worksheets, give an example of all the steps to complete similar math problems.

- Allow plenty of workspace on each worksheet for answering all the steps of a math problem.

- Number each step needed. This way the student will know how many steps are actually needed to find the answer.

- Type all teacher-prepared worksheets, assignments and tests in text size 14.

- Check all teacher-prepared worksheets, assignments and tests for "readability"; Does it make sense, and is it easy to follow? If dyslexic students don't understand the question, it will be impossible for them to answer with understanding and confidence. In other words, they'll just guess instead.

- Avoid using double-negatives (such as except, not, nor, or other than) for math problem sentences in worksheets, assignments and tests. Trick questions are not necessary and do nothing to verify understanding.

- Put the decimal point in red ink. It helps with visual perception.

- Use a brain based lesson format—warm up with mental math and visual notation, problem solve with teacher explanation and guided oral problem solving, and cool down by playing games with math.

- Have students count objects, starting at 100 and working backwards.

- Encourage students to cook at home so they can become more familiar with measurements.

- Involve students in measuring the height of classmates.

- Have students create a budget on how their allowance money is to be spent.

- Read "story problems" aloud to student and check for understanding.

- Use math puzzles and games to gain student interest in new math concepts.

- Make learning math fun!

Joseph age 10

"It's a poor mind that can only
think of one way to spell a word."

-Andrew Jackson
7th President of the United
States of America

Writing and Spelling

It is not uncommon for children with dyslexia to have poor handwriting, misspelled or crossed out words, incorrect/missing punctuation or incomplete sentences or paragraph conclusions in their writing. Weaknesses in visual memory are the cause for "common word" deficits in children with dyslexia, which is why they have trouble remembering what the words "look" like. They have difficulty selecting and holding thoughts long enough to write them down.

Accessible accommodations in writing and spelling are necessary for children with dyslexia and should include the following:

- Always explain the "three parts of a word"—what it looks like, what it sounds like and what it means.

- Accept that interesting words spelled incorrectly are of greater value than boring words spelled correctly.

- When marking for spelling or grammar, adopt the "less is more" approach and "feed forward." Tell the student how to do it next time rather what they've done wrong now.

- Do not negatively focus on handwriting/penmanship. Neat handwriting is difficult for dyslexic students. Overemphasizing neatness can detract from the student strengths in equally or more important areas.

- Allow dyslexic students to use a computer and spell check for written assignments.

- Be flexible in ways a dyslexic student can show what they know and how they gather information.

- Encourage students to read their writing from right to left (instead of left to right) as a strategy for spotting spelling errors.

- Before a writing assignment, provide the student with a list of "trigger" words that might be used to describe an event or a chapter from a book. Trigger words help the student visualize what to write.

- Have the student create a "dictionary" book of new words learned.

- Improve punctuation ability by providing the student with five or six typewritten sentences without any punctuation, omitting uppercase letters and periods, and ask the student to punctuate the passage into sentences and capitalize where appropriate.

- Establish a "Post Office" in the classroom and provide students with opportunities to write, mail, and receive letters to and from their classmates, teacher(s), principal, librarian, sports coaches, parents, grandparents and other family members.

- Encourage students to express themselves freely during free writing/journal writing time, without fear of being graded down for spelling errors. Instead, instruct the student to merely circle words they are not sure are correct and the teacher will assist in helping to erase and correct them later.

- Create a master spelling list of words from books being read. Then estimate how many words (maybe two or three) the student will be able to learn in one spelling session, introducing one new word each day or every other day.

- Communicate regularly with the student's parents concerning strategies to rehearse spelling words at home.

- Use the talk to write method. The student talks through their thoughts aloud, repeating as necessary, until their thoughts are clear enough to begin writing.

- Use visual, auditory, tactile and kinesthetic teaching activities for how the student sees the word, hears the word read, reads the word, studies individual letters and letter combinations, hears the word pronounced by syllables and phonemes, hears the word spelled, orally spells the word, copies the word in the air while saying each letter, traces the word with fingers while saying the letter names, copies the word on paper, and spells the word from memory.

Olivia age 11

"Cleaning your house while your children are growing, is like shoveling snow while it's still snowing."

-Phyllis Diller
Comedian/actress

Organization

Even non-dyslexics have trouble organizing their day. Many students have problems with organization, such as difficulty remembering what to do for homework, holding onto (and not losing) assignments once completed and filing papers in proper order for future reference. Organizational deficits with dyslexic students can include difficulties with:

- Allocating and organizing time.

- Setting priorities, time management and estimating time.

- Solving problems in stages.

- Remembering what to do.

- Arranging/locating the beginning, middle and end of a task.

- Organizing desks/notebooks or searching for materials.

- Drafting an outline or assembling materials for presentations.

Teaching organizational skills requires written step-by-step instruction and consistency in using those learned skills. Here are some suggestions:

- Ensure a "clutter free" desk/workspace to complete in-class assignments.

- Periodically have the students sort through and clean out their desks, book bags/backpacks and other designated places where completed assignments are kept.

- Provide an assignment notebook to help organize homework and future projects.

- Teach students to read time and/or use a wristwatch to manage their time when completing assigned work.

- Teach the students how to use a calendar to schedule their assignments and due dates, including when to start and how to break the assignment into smaller steps for easier progress monitoring.

- Prepare a written daily classroom schedule of planned activities and place where the student can visually review the schedule throughout the class day.

- Create a reward system for having an organized desk, organized schoolwork/assignments, etc.

- Create a daily to do list of items to complete and in a particular order. Children with dyslexia have difficulty understanding the proper order of a task. The to do list or checklist needs to remain in constant sight of the dyslexic student. If the list is inside a notebook, the student will first have to remember to look inside the notebook to see the list—which probably won't happen. The key is to be able to see the list, which is the visual prompt to actually use the list.

- Observe the student's organizational skills and offer suggestions as needed.

- Provide a clear plastic letter-sized envelope to be used for completing and/or turning in completed homework. This reduces the possibility that homework will go missing.

Hanna age 8

"Slow down and everything you are
chasing will come around and catch you."

-John de Paola
Author

Pace Reduction

Busy classroom schedules can sometimes be overwhelming for students and their teacher(s), and in most instances the day ends less productive and needing more work. This is because the typical student "tunes out" when the load becomes too heavy and goals for completion seem too difficult to attain.

Dyslexic students struggle even more, because they need a slower (not faster) pace to process information. Dyslexic students often misinterpret spoken language when the classroom pace and instruction is too fast.

When teachers take more time to assure student understanding and match pacing to their needs, students—whether dyslexic or non-dyslexic—benefit.

Slowing down and pacing classroom instruction to meet the needs of each student occurs naturally when patience and empathy are more valued than lesson content.

By understanding that dyslexics have a difficult time processing, prioritizing and remembering long lists of directions at one time, teachers can proactively do the following:

- Provide one direction at a time. By doing so, the dyslexic student does not have to process multiple steps at one time, assuring better results and reducing repeating of directions.

- Teach one concept at a time, while drawing connections with prior knowledge. This helps the dyslexic student make neural connections that confirm better understanding.

- Provide visual representation of oral instruction, which will promote a more evenly paced learning environment. Dyslexics are more right-brain dominant and need more multi-sensory instruction that engages multiple areas of the non-dominant (left) side of brain to make new brain connections and better remember information.

- Preview each new concept before instruction. By doing so, dyslexic students can better organize, filter and prioritize new information. Previewing engages students into what is to come and focuses their attention.

- Review each new concept before moving on. This helps the dyslexic student more effectively connect, categorize and store information that was just presented. Reviewing helps to build upon understanding before moving on. Reviewing and learning at a more even pace is better for all students.

- Pause often. Allow the dyslexic student more time to respond (with teacher encouragement and prompts) when answering teacher questions.

- Keep instruction novel. Avoid performing the same activity over and over for a long time. Vary activities each class time to spur interest and deter boredom.

- Take a few deep breaths and slow down. Racing towards a red light doesn't do anyone any good.

Paulina age 13

"No one knows how children will turn out. A great tree often springs from a tender plant."

-Proverb

Extended Time

Teachers often predetermine in-class school work and homework assignments based on an estimate of how much time it will take students to complete work. Timeframes are typically calculated on class average performance levels, which do not include considerations for dyslexic students. This is problematic for children with dyslexia because it can take them two to three times longer to complete the same assignment (no kidding). Accessibility to education should include:

- Extended time to complete assignments. Allow the dyslexic student "extra specified time," providing a different date to turn in an assignment.

- It is important that all extensions of time be pre-planned, to head off stress from any extemporaneous approvals.

Allowing time to process basic skills, such as reading and writing, can sometimes leave insufficient time to demonstrate ability in other areas, such as storytelling, problem solving and comprehension. The following adjustments in time in the classroom are extremely helpful:

- Post visual predetermined timeframe parameters (such as 10 minutes of instruction, 15 minutes of discussion and 20 minutes of group or individual work).

- Provide an overview of the topic and goal achieved by a specific time or date.

- Allow extra thinking time by exploring the unexplained (query) during discussion time.

- Be less concerned about teaching to the clock time and concentrate more on the rhythm of learning time needed.

- Pause often during instruction and ask intriguing questions that engage students in different ways; humor works.

- Apply a short break (transition time) between changes in curriculum. Allow students to organize previously completed work into their folders/binders, etc. before introducing new material.

- Announce early when homework is due, and not when the school bell is ringing and the teacher is shouting instructions as they leave. (Picture for a moment, the chaos and noise during class changes.)

- Allow non-timed testing or divide the test into two parts on different days, with teacher as proctor.

- Be consistent when allocating extra time so that the dyslexic student can anticipate pre-planned teacher scheduling.

- Remember that dyslexic students have to work two to three times as hard (requiring up to five times more energy) as non-dyslexics, just to keep up with the rest of the class and that they are mentally exhausted by the end of the school day.

- Be patient with time and do not become frustrated. Accept that every student learns differently and be flexible in teaching style.

- Request help from school administration if the amount of extended time necessary for the dyslexic student becomes difficult to manage, thereby eliminating any disruption in student learning.

Lila age 9

"I liked homework better
when it was called coloring."

-Anonymous

Homework

By the end of a school day, children with dyslexia are generally more tired (mentally fatigued) than their peers. This is because everything requires far more effort and thought, tasks take longer to complete and nothing comes easily. Children with dyslexia need three to four times as long as their peers (yes, really!) to complete homework and therefore, not be penalized for not finishing homework in the same timeframe or format. Appropriate accessibility that improves positive homework outcomes include:

Checking homework:

- Writing homework on the board at the beginning of class.

- Allowing plenty of time for students to write down homework.

- Checking that homework notes are correctly written, or providing pre-printed teacher notes or handouts.

- Providing student with a "homework buddy."

Modifying homework:

- Reducing the amount of homework (fewer questions, math problems and written work) or having the student complete every other or every third question.

- Reducing the number of pages to read from a book.

- Setting the amount of time required for homework. Whether they have finished or not, the student should stop when they have reached the time limit.

- Planning with other teachers the length and frequency of homework assignments and adopting homework practices for their students with dyslexia.

Accepting different homework applications and formats:

- Allowing use of illustrations, handmade models/artwork, power presentation, dramatization, poetry, music lyrics, or other creative ways to represent completed homework.

- Allowing homework be completed using a computer.

- Providing an extra textbook to be left at home—the other at school, designated for student use in the classroom.

Communicating:

- Providing weekly feedback to parents on student progress, homework completion and/or recommendations for further interventions. Agree on a day of the week for communicating.

- Giving frequent reminders about due dates. Have student write due dates on front page of all worksheets and assignments.

- Creating a reward system for in school work and homework completed.

- Allowing/encouraging "extra credit" for extra work on assignments in which the student shows high interest.

- Being consistent when collecting homework and immediately notifying the student if an assignment is not turned in.

- Posting homework assignments/instructions on school/teacher website.

- Setting homework at the start of a lesson and reminding again at the end.

- Explaining the purpose of the homework assignment and ensuring student understanding.

- Reviewing homework promptly and providing immediate feedback or instructions as needed.

- Planning with the student's other teachers, the length and frequency of homework assignments and adopting similar/consistent homework practices that benefit the student.

Oliver age 16

"The day you're willing to veer off
the lesson plan, follow a kid's lead,
and learn with your students, is the
day you really become a teacher."

-Anonymous

Methods of Marking and Grading

It is soul-destroying for a dyslexic student be handed back an assignment or test covered in red marks and negative comments, yet this is something they experience almost every school day.

Eventually, the dyslexic student will begin finding ways to prevent or avoid the emotional pain they experience from each red mark and negative comment, by:

- Doing the homework but not turning it in to the teacher.

- Throwing out schoolwork that is negatively marked before their parents review it.

- Saying homework was completed when it was never done.

- Deliberately losing homework or having missing pages.

In essence, the dyslexic student begins hiding a learning disability they don't even know they have.

Since no one (parents/teachers) understands what the dyslexic student is coping with, the problem gets worse. Teachers and parents begin reprimanding the dyslexic student for incomplete or missing schoolwork. And because the student has not been evaluated for a learning disability, they believe the student is not motivated and/or is lazy. Such behavior creates a vicious circle that the dyslexic student cannot understand, communicate or control.

Until the student is formally identified with a learning disability, the problem will go unattended and unresolved. Grades will continue to drop, the student's self-esteem will suffer and a downward spiral of educational failure will take center stage.

It is imperative that parents be pro-active in requesting that their child be evaluated for a learning disability and that they see it through to the educational support needed.

Appropriate marking and grading for dyslexic students equals accessibility in education, and it should include the following:

- Mark for content, rather than spelling, grammar or punctuation. Concentrate on what is correct. Children with dyslexia have persistent problems with sentence structure, punctuation and organization of written work, which is not due to lack of academic experience.

- Focus on "big picture" success. Encourage thinking, not just reading accuracy. In the right context, "butifull" (misspelled) is better than "nice" (spelled correctly). Children with dyslexia sometimes have difficulty "seeing" their own spelling errors, but they may correctly spell the word orally.

- Mark schoolwork in a positive way. Praising for effort is just as important as praising for achievement. Lightly underline or use a dot (not an "x" or red ink) to highlight spelling errors.

- Identify successes in the student's schoolwork—the "wow" factor, such as, "Fantastic, you are "spot on!"

- Avoid negative comments. A student's emotional response to negativity does not enable reflection or improvement. Children with dyslexia sometimes have difficulty "reading between the lines" of adverse criticism.

- Provide positive suggestions with ideas that pique their interest and encourage participation.

- Avoid double negatives or comments on what "should not" be done. Use simple comments to say what "should" be done, which is easier to process and understand.

- Offer incentives to encourage student success.

- Emphasize/evaluate oral performance assignment options over written assignments.

- Focus on the student's ideas. Focus on what the student is trying to say, rather than on any errors.

- Concentrate on understanding the point, even if there are mistakes in the text.

- Do not criticize forgotten knowledge. Children with dyslexia have compromised short-term working memory and therefore forget things easily.

- Print legibly any teacher comments. At the same time, no comments at all (silence) is unacceptable. All student schoolwork deserves acknowledgement.

- Return graded assignments and tests within three working days from submission. Dyslexic students need immediate feedback as to how well they're doing. Parents can monitor their child's progress more effectively and help them self-correct future assignments.

Timothy age 14

"I failed my way to success."

-Thomas Edison
American inventor

Testing

Tests are to measure what students know, not what they don't know. A dyslexic student may have difficulty demonstrating mastery by writing an essay but may have more success with a fill-in-the-blank or multiple choice test.

Tests need "accessibility" to children with dyslexia. A test that does not include accommodations and/or modifications is not accessible. To be accessible to children with dyslexia, testing needs to:

- Provide a vocabulary list/word bank.

- Be fill-in-the-blank, matching, circle the correct answer or true false formats, rather than all multiple choice or essay style.

- Provide test review sheets prior to testing (front loading).

- Provide study guides with answers.

- Allow more time or non-timed testing, with short breaks.

- Allow oral testing.

- Accept poor grammar and spelling mistakes.

- Avoid trick questions, double negatives and mixed messages on test questions.

- Underline key words such as at, after, or not.

- Underline and highlight key words in negative questions, such as "Which country is **not** in North America?"

- Avoid essay-type questions as much as possible. (Essay questions will take dyslexic students longer to complete.)

- Provide an explanation/definition for words, in order to define, clarify or identify, or else simplify test wording, rephrase test questions and/or rephrase directions.

- Clarify (teacher/proctor) any particular questions the dyslexic student may have during the exam.

- Offer different test formats, such as computer, PowerPoint, visual presentations, skills demonstrations, open book tests or open note tests.

- Specify when essay-writing tests have more than one instruction. Notate the numeric actions/steps. State the number of lines, paragraphs or pages required.

- Accept short answers.

- Provide a private exam room with a test proctor.

- Offer extra credit options.

- Alternate ways to assess student knowledge, such as via projects or oral presentations instead of written tests.

- Preview (teacher/proctor) the test processing with the student.

- Allow use of calculator or word processor/spell check.

- Place fewer questions or problems on each page.

- Provide "typed" test materials (same font, text size 14), with more spacing between words and sentences.

- Discuss (teacher/proctor) the test format ahead of time.

- Provide (teacher/proctor) reading support during test.

- Provide a shorter test and/or break the test into smaller parts.

- Use multiple-choice tests, instead of short-answer or essay tests.

- Use visual aids or drawings, reducing the amount of reading required.

- Offer "open book" exams, reducing memorization problems.

- Summarize the most important ideas with concept cards.

- Review (teacher/proctor) material with concept cards.

- Eliminate "machine-readable" answer sheets and allow student to write on test sheet instead.

- Not require student to copy or write exam questions on exam sheet first, before the test.

- Be aware (teacher) of overall test readability, making sure test questions are easily understood and rephrasing test content and/or simplifying wording when appropriate.

- Avoid handwritten tests.

- Provide practice tests.

- Before testing, conduct a personal review with the student to verify understanding of a topic.

- Re-read to students any test questions that require extra exposure.

- Conduct periodic short question and answer sessions throughout the teaching process, giving student feedback as to their understanding of a particular topic.

- Use spelling words that test knowledge of specific features, and not just typical vocabulary or subject content.

- Require fewer responses when grading.

- Avoid "pop" quizzes.

- Alternate options for demonstrating learning.

- Provide test times that are preplanned, to avoid extemporaneous decisions that negatively impact and stress the student on test days.

Jessica age 12

"Some people are carbon copies.
Others make their own impression."

-Anonymous

Copying and Note Taking

Note taking or classroom board copying is rarely taught as part of school learning. However, because of their complex nature, copying and note taking are often difficult tasks for the dyslexic student. When copying, dyslexic students will often lose their place and become frustrated while trying to focus on the teacher's written notes.

Learned language skills of reading, letter formation (handwriting), spelling and working memory are required for accurate copying or note taking. For dyslexics with reading, writing and spelling difficulties, the simplest copying/note taking activities become extremely difficult, confusing and fatiguing. Spelling errors, word substitutions and omissions are common.

There are two types of academic copying: (a) Copying from the "far" point and (b) copying from the "near" point. Any copy work done from the board or lecture copying is "far" point copying. Copying from a textbook or computer interface document is "near" point copying. Both types of copying need the following accommodations to help the dyslexic student:

- "Near" point copying should be in 14 point text size, and easy to read font (Century Gothic, Arial and Avenir) and 1.5 line spacing. Different fonts and sizes within the same document are confusing, cluttered looking and difficult to follow.

- Teacher-written board notes should be clearly printed, with an awareness of writing style and letter formation. The writing should be large enough to see from the back of the classroom, avoiding combination print/writing, abbreviations, small scribbling or incomplete directions. Keep instructions short and to the point. Allow generous spacing between each line and make punctuation bold to emphasize the ending of the sentence and instruction.

- Do not have the dyslexic student re-write attempted note taking, as a form of punishment.

- Provide student with teacher-written notes at the end of class or provide teacher notes ahead of time so that the student is able to follow the classroom instruction more readily.

- Allow plenty of time for note taking and board copying. "Near" and "far" point copying should occur early during class time, rather than waiting until near the end of the class and requiring students to rush their copying of board notes.

- Leave board notes on the board throughout class time.

- Use fill-in-the blank instruction note taking sheets to build note taking skills.

- Allow students enough time to copy notes from board without verbal interruption/over talking. Dyslexic students have difficulty copying from the board and listening to teacher instruction at the same time.

- Before moving on, check to make sure that the dyslexic student has copied everything correctly from the board.

- Allow the dyslexic student a clear view of the board.

- For left-handed students with dyslexia, placement of word lists should be written at the "right" margin (not the left).

- Allow plenty of line-spaced paper for answers or notes.

- Numerically specify the order and sequence of instruction.

- Utilize "thin notes"—handouts containing text down the center of the page with large side margins, used for "picture thinkers" to draw diagrams or for "word thinkers" to note or summarize main points.

- Allow dyslexic students to type classroom instruction and/or board notes on a classroom computer/laptop, etc.

- Mathematical note taking is extremely challenging for the dyslexic student. Teachers should give the dyslexic student copies of their notes or outline of master textbook math problems and exercises.

Arthur age 11

"The whole purpose of education
is to turn mirrors into windows."

-Sydney J. Harris
American Journalist

Format of Reading Materials, Worksheets, Assignments and Tests

Presenting information in a format that makes it easily accessible (readable) is vital for children with dyslexia. While reading, the shape and size of words dictate how well they process information.

Children with dyslexia often experience visual discomfort when reading, which disturbs concentration and makes the problem worse. The following educational accommodations will help relieve the pressures of visual discomfort and improve readability:

- Use font style Avenir, Century Gothic or Arial. Do not use different font styles or text sizes on the same page.

- Modify text size to 12 or 14 (depending on the font) with 1.5 line spacing.

- Use block style layout (no first-line paragraph indents), with left margin justified and right margin "ragged" (not justified).

- Avoid overcrowding. Too much text on the page overloads the dyslexic student's visual working memory and has a negative effect on brain focus.

- Avoid columns and divided (hyphenated) words.

- Highlight (bold) key words and headings only. Avoid italics.

- Provide ample spacing between each question.

- Depending upon the question, allow a generous amount of space for answering.

- Use lined-spacing for answering questions.

- Use only one side of the paper for assignments and tests.

- Print assignments or tests on "off white" (non-glaring) paper.

- Organize assignments or tests by "clustering" or "chunking" information and/or concepts. This offers more focus and less confusion to the student.

- Design test questions and/or assignments around a given conclusion or fact. Be specific as to what the student is to think about.

- Do not use open end questions that can have many answers.

- Avoid using mixed messages, double negatives or trick questions on assignments, worksheets and tests.

- Organize test questions so that only one question is being asked at a time.

- Avoid asking multiple questions for multiple answers in one test question.

- Notate the numeric actions/steps necessary to complete each question and answer.

- Use diagrams and illustrations to break up large sections of text.

- Depending upon the length, separate assignments or tests into two sessions.

- Use clear, unambiguous pictures with key words or short sentences.

- Avoid "busy" worksheets with speech bubbles, diagrams or drawings.

- Use off-white, cream-colored or light-grey matt paper to reduce glare and eyestrain.

- Use numbers or bullet points, rather than continuous prose.

- Avoid using background graphics ("watermarks") on written text sheets.

- Check readability of teacher-provided worksheets so that the dyslexic student will be able to read them easily.

A CHILD'S TOUCHSTONE

"To get all that life wants for you, apply what I call the Boomerang Effect: Give out what you most want to see come back."

-Robin Sharma, Canadian writer

Anais age 7

"Iron rusts from disuse; water loses its purity from stagnation…even so does inaction sap the vigor of my mind."

-Leonardo da Vinci
High Renaissance Italian Painter

CHAPTER 36

Learning through Movement

Young children rarely stay still, except when they're sleeping. They are constantly moving about—running, jumping, stretching and challenging every muscle in their small bodies. For them, sitting still in one place is unnatural. They prefer lying face down on the ground while observing something new, or face up when observing the shapes of clouds in the sky. Their lives are more connected to everyday things, like a butterfly on a flower, a fawn nibbling on sweet grass or a whisper of wind that gently passes across their face. To them, life is a constant flow of brilliant light.

This changes however, when young children begin school. Suddenly their lives are in an upright position. No longer are they learning by rolling down hills, climbing trees or spinning in circles. The adult world expects them to sit still, focus, and do as they're instructed, all without difficulty and complaint. Really?

Even when society tries to make them stay still, nothing really does. Observe children in a classroom and you will know this is true. Their movement is constant, like a slowmoving stream, synchronizing sounds around them, all the while learning, even when the adults around them see something different.

Movement while learning not only enhances the experience <u>but</u> is essential to the learning process. Without it, learning can be boring. Just ask any student who enjoys hands-on activities versus reading to learn from only a book.

Every day, students unintentionally "zone out" during class. Teachers find themselves constantly asking students to focus and pay attention, but to no avail. Frustration builds and exasperated teachers don't know what to do.

The solution is as simple as allowing students movement within the classroom. No matter what the grade level, students learn better when they can move, dialogue and collaborate with others. Sound familiar?

Why is it, then, that most classroom environments insist on students' sitting still and paying attention, when the opposite is natural? Think about it. Most adults would balk at the mere suggestion that they are not allowed to speak unless spoken to, suggest a new idea only when called upon or disagree in jeopardy of being fired. That's called a dictatorship, which rarely survives in the free world.

So how do teachers change the classroom environment from sedentary discipline to motivating action? By being more interesting, different and better than other teachers.

Successful movement in the classroom includes:

- Cueing the music and start dancing. Music and dance open student minds in miraculous ways. Add quiz questions for impromptu answers and see amazing results.

- Exercise. Have students do wall push-ups (set to dramatic, uplifting music) before completing inclass assignments. Not only is this fun for the students, but the teacher will enjoy setting an uplifting tone.

- Dance to the oldies. Classics such as "Let's Do the Twist" by Chubby Checker, "Jump" by Van Halen, the theme song from Rocky and even a country's national anthem can inspire movement.

- Create an indoor obstacle course that results in finding the answer to a question.

- Include student ideas that encourage movement activities while learning new material.

- Surprise students with clues within the classroom that need out-of-the-box thinking to solve and find the treasure, while incorporating mathematical problem solving.

  Teachers who incorporate movement into their daily classroom curriculum usually have happier students, which can encourage, support and improve academic results. Children with dyslexia are naturally drawn to movement and music because it enhances their learning experience.

Charlotte age 8

"Play is often talked about as if it were
a relief from serious learning. But for
children, play is serious learning. Play
is really the work of childhood."

-"Mr. Fred Rogers"
American Educator, Minister, Songwriter,
Author and Television Host

CHAPTER 37

Physical Activity and Team Sports

There's nothing more fun than playing. Children are experts at knowing what makes them happiest, which is why anything that requires movement, including physical activity and team sports, is at the top of their list.

For some children, however, having fun by playing sports is conditional and predicated on first completing all homework assignments, paying attention in class and getting average to above average passing grades. Some schools have very specific rules before a student can participate in team sports, including natural ability. In other words, if students are unable to play a sport as well as other players, they are "cut" from the team. Schools use the excuse that there are only a specific number of positions available and everyone must "try out." Only the best performing students will make the team.

High school sports typically include students from four grade levels (ninth through twelfth). A ninth grade student who wants to try out for a sport has to compete with students who have already been on the team for one to three years. For these schools, if a student doesn't already have previous experience at playing the desired sport and can compete for a place, rarely do they make the team.

Most parents find these rules not only wrong but unfair, while other parents expect their student's school to have a "winning team" and believe that cutting underperformers is part of the process.

Some school athletic/sport coaches believe that being cut from a team "builds character." Most students however, are emotionally devastated. To most students, it doesn't feel "character building" at all; it tells them that according to the coach, they're not good enough. To counteract this response, coaches will suggest they can try out again next year, while directing the student to regular physical education, but without participation on a school team.

Some schools and athletic/sport coaches believe that all schools, both public and private, function the same way. They are wrong. Many public and private schools offer club and/or "intramural" sports. This means that every student, at every level, plays their desired sport. They believe children develop their abilities at different stages in their lives and that athletic ability is not predetermined by a "tryout."

For these public and private schools and parents, most important is whether their child/student is able to play and be a part of the team. Sport coaches who encourage positive athletic contributions by all students wanting to play team sports, are to be commended.

Children with learning disabilities, especially those with dyslexia, are often denied sport team participation. They're told they lack motivation and are not living up to their academic potential. It is the opinion of some schools and athletic/sport coaches that students with dyslexia do not need special education support. They believe that sport-team requirements do not negatively affect students with dyslexia. They are wrong!

Children with dyslexia who are not evaluated or who are denied special education services and/support are at a dual disadvantage: (a) Their grades are slipping, and they are blamed for not living up to their potential, and (b) they're denied participation in team sports because their grade point average (GPA) is below school requirements.

Most educational experts who work with dyslexic children agree that physical activities, such as team sports, are especially beneficial for those with dyslexia. Playing sports normalizes their experience, letting them be like other kids, improving a positive image and academic performance.

Team sports can also improve relationships with teachers. Watching their student playing a team sport, the teacher may more likely view him/her as a whole person rather than just a struggling student.

Most school aged children just want to play and be part of the team. It's their right as a child.

Tyson age 10

"Do not train a child to learn by force or harshness; but direct them to it by what amuses their minds, so that you may be better able to discover with accuracy the peculiar bent of the genius of each."

-Plato

CHAPTER 38

Accommodation Action Plan

It's no secret that the majority of academic learning occurs in the classrooms of general education teachers. Special education "pull out" times for students with learning disabilities, such as dyslexia, rarely occur, if at all. Because of this, today's classroom teachers require more training in teaching students with learning differences and addressing their academic challenges.

Teachers who are not properly trained on specific learning disabilities, such as dyslexia, may not be as vested or committed to the belief that instructional and non-instructional accommodations will be effective in addressing the student's needs. Instead, they remain frustrated with some of their students.

Simply put, teachers are misinformed if they choose not to provide instructional and non-instructional accommodations to a struggling student because they believe an evaluation must be performed first.

Properly trained teachers intuitively know when a student is struggling academically due to a learning disability, even before a formal evaluation validates their concerns.

A teacher's gut feeling and desire to immediately employ instructional and non-instructional accommodations to help a student, trumps waiting for testing and evaluation results before doing anything.

No laws state that teachers are prohibited from providing accommodations to students, prior to or during a special education evaluation. In fact, documented results of accommodations provided prior to an evaluation can help in determining appropriate accommodations for a student's Individual Accommodation Plan (IEP).

The following Individual Accommodation Plan will help guide teachers and parents in providing instructional and non-instructional accommodations to students with dyslexia and/or other specific learning disabilities.

Individual Accommodation Plan for Students Identified with Dyslexia/ Reading Disorder/SLD

Name of Student: _____

Grade: _____ Subject: _____ Teacher: _____

In order to support the academic needs of _____,
the following accommodations have been identified as the best
ways to teach and support _____ (his/her) learning style:

Classroom Environment:

☐ With student understanding and permission, relocate desk seating closer to teacher instruction. This does not necessarily mean the student should be in the front row, but the student should be within close proximity for teacher assistance.

☐ Devise a non-verbal "hand signal" the student can use to indicate student assistance is needed. The teacher can then visit with the student without over-attention from others.

☐ Provide clear (with proper pronunciation), even-toned (calm and patient), slower-paced verbal instruction, in order to reduce classroom anxiety.

☐ Reward accuracy and effort. For the student acquiring an academic skill who is not yet proficient, provide encouragement and/or incentives for overall effort and accuracy for any work completed, rather than focusing on speed or full completion of work.

☐ Pause often, and allow the student more time to respond (with teacher encouragement and prompts) when answering teacher questions. Remember to smile and react positively.

(Continued on the next page)

- ☐ Pre-notify the student when activities are about to change. Give a five-minute "heads up" to the student, thereby reducing anxiety and/or frustration during transition.

- ☐ Provide the student with brief, regular, repeated doses of positive adult attention (scheduled attention) to encourage and confirm a positive direction in the schoolwork.

- ☐ Set an "appropriate tone" in the classroom. All students should feel comfortable, safe from ridicule, teasing, chuckling or laughter during oral class discussion or reading.

- ☐ Use a "brain-based" lesson format. Warm up with mental, visual and auditory senses, and problem-solve with teacher explanation and guided oral problem solving.

- ☐ Preview new topics or concepts first, before introducing new materials or lessons. This allows the dyslexic student time to mentally prepare for new information.

- ☐ Review each topic or concept just taught. This helps the student connect, categorize and process information just presented. Be prepared to provide a demonstration or concrete example to accompany an oral explanation.

- ☐ Ensure that the student is included and part of group projects by organizing student groups in advance. Do not allow other students to decide who may or may not be part of their group.

- ☐ Avoid habituation (non-associative learning in which repeated exposure to the same stimulus, topic or teaching method leads to decreased responses). By keeping instruction novel, student attention stays more engaged and focused.

- ☐ Other: _____

- ☐ Other: _____

(Continued on the next page)

Teacher Instruction:

- ☐ Teacher to confirm student understanding of directions, lesson plans and homework before end of class day.

- ☐ Written board instructions are to be clearly printed (no script/print combination writing or abbreviations). Allow enough time for the student to accurately write instructions, which is followed by teacher confirmation that the instructions are written and understood.

- ☐ If needed, teacher to provide a different (variable) explanation to instructions until clarified and understood by the student. Repeat instruction (slowly), as needed, for further clarification. (Do not assume that the student understands without confirmation and verification by the teacher.)

- ☐ Teacher to rely less on textbooks and more on activities that make reading and reading-by-learning assignments more interesting and relevant. Teacher will combine seeing, saying, writing and doing activities into lessons.

- ☐ Provide ways student can "visually think" about what is being discussed.

- ☐ Allow student to explore all possible answers and methods to what is being taught.

- ☐ Allow student to "work backwards" through the question to find answers. Be flexible of the process.

- ☐ Use a variety of materials, current events, and hands-on applications to teach student understanding.

- ☐ Increase the student's fund of knowledge and expose student to newspapers, magazines, television documentaries and news programs. Provide opportunities to discuss information presented.

(Continued on the next page)

- ☐ Provide teacher-printed notes for announcements of future work projects/assignments. (Note: The student will not be able to remember verbal assignment instructions.)

- ☐ Provide example(s) on steps to complete assignments.

- ☐ While teaching, explain the "three parts of a word"—what it looks like, what it sounds like, and what it means.

- ☐ Encourage and compliment student oral expression and presentation.

- ☐ Be patient with student responses. Children with dyslexia can be highly articulate but often have to search for words, which gives the mistaken impression they are unsure of what they're trying to say.

- ☐ Be flexible in ways the student can show what they know and how they gather information.

- ☐ Provide one instruction at a time. By doing so, the student doesn't have to process multiple steps at one time, assuring better results and reducing the repeating of directions.

- ☐ Teach one concept at a time, while drawing connections to prior knowledge. This helps the student make neural connections that confirm better understanding.

- ☐ Pause often during instruction and ask intriguing questions that engage student in different ways.

- ☐ Provide positive suggestions with ideas that pique their interest and encourage participation.

- ☐ Avoid double negatives or comments on what "not" to do. Use simple comments that say what "should" be done, which is easier to process and understand.

- ☐ Use "hands on" manipulatives and activities (kinesthetic) for student learning.

(Continued on the next page)

- ☐ Focus on the student's ideas. Focus on what the student is trying to say, rather than on any errors.

- ☐ Identify successes in the student's schoolwork. The "wow" factor, such as "Fantastic, you're spot on!"

- ☐ Prepare copy of notes summarizing content from a class lecture or assigned reading, with blanks inserted in the notes where key facts or concepts should appear. As information is covered during lecture or in a reading assignment, the student writes missing content into blanks to complete the guided notes.

- ☐ Provide a copy of class notes to allow the student to focus more fully on the lecture and class discussion. This strategy can be strengthened by requiring the student to highlight key vocabulary terms appearing in the prepared notes as they are brought up in the lecture or discussion.

- ☐ Do not criticize forgotten knowledge. Children with dyslexia have compromised short-term working-memory issues.

- ☐ Allow student to choose reading material of interest, when the activity is reading for pleasure.

- ☐ Use fun visuals and simulations when introducing new material. Children with dyslexia are "picture thinkers" and need both visual and auditory senses stimulated.

- ☐ Offer incentives to encourage student success.

- ☐ Other: _____

- ☐ Other: _____

(Continued on the next page)

Assignments and Homework:

- ☐ Provide a list of required readings and arrange to obtain textbooks/books on CD/tape/e-books well in advance of need.

- ☐ Provide advance notice of oral class reading, including the passage or paragraph to be read.

- ☐ Accept family reading (between student and family member) as "minutes read per day" reading credit.

- ☐ Allow student to draw illustrations or build models to explain an assignment or project.

- ☐ Offer student a choice, such as reading a passage independently or discussing the passage in a group learning activity.

- ☐ Offer student a choice of task sequence. When the student has several tasks to complete during independent work, allow the student to select the order in which he/she will complete those tasks. When the student begins the independent work, provide encouragement, prompting and time management as needed to keep the student engaged.

- ☐ Allow student to use a computer and spell and grammar check for written assignments.

- ☐ Provide a list of "trigger" words that might be used to complete a written assignment.

- ☐ Do not negatively focus on handwriting/penmanship.

- ☐ Do not mark down for misspelled words. Accept that interesting words spelled incorrectly are of more value than boring words spelled correctly.

- ☐ Provide an assignment notebook to help organize homework and future projects.

- ☐ Provide a clear, plastic, letter-size envelope to be used for completing and/or turning in completed homework.

(Continued on the next page)

- ☐ Allow extended time to complete assignments by providing a different turn-in date, boldly noted on the worksheet.

- ☐ Announce/write on board early, when homework is due (prior to end of class).

- ☐ Explain the purpose of the homework and the outcome of understanding the assignment.

- ☐ Check that homework notes are correctly written, or provide pre-printed teacher notes or handouts, with due dates.

- ☐ Review homework, grade and provide feedback to student within three days of receipt.

- ☐ Provide copies of teacher written and instruction notes.

- ☐ Organize assignments by "clustering" or "chunking" information and/or concepts, which offers more focus and less confusion to the student.

- ☐ Design assignments around a given conclusion or fact. Be specific as to what the student is to think about.

- ☐ Avoid using open-ended questions that can have many answers.

- ☐ Reduce number of homework problems (complete only odd-numbered or even-numbered problems).

- ☐ Notate numeric actions/steps necessary to complete each task and/or assignment.

- ☐ Share weekly listings of upcoming homework assignments with the student. Also, ensure these homework assignments are shared with the student's parent(s), to help them support their child's homework completion.

- ☐ Check readability of teacher-provided worksheets so the student can read and understand them easily.

- ☐ Other: _____

- ☐ Other: _____

(Continued on the next page)

Testing:

☐ Front-load: Prior to testing, provide test review sheets or study guide.

☐ Allow "open book" exams, thereby reducing memorization problems.

☐ Provide practice tests/study guides with answers.

☐ Allow more time or non-timed testing.

☐ Provide oral testing, rather than written testing.

☐ Read test questions to student.

☐ Arrange for another student to be the dyslexic student's study buddy. Offer incentives for studying together prior to tests.

☐ Provide typed tests (not handwritten ones), using text size 14, with one font style only; no italics.

☐ Offer different test formats (computer, PowerPoint, visual presentations/demonstration of skills, open-book tests).

☐ Provide an explanation/definition for words, such as define, clarify or identify, or simplify test wording by rephrasing test questions and/or directions.

☐ Specify when essay-writing tests have more than one instruction. Notate the numeric actions/steps. State the number of lines, paragraphs or pages required.

☐ Provide ample lined spaces for answering essay questions.

☐ Give student a choice; for the graded point(s), offer more than one essay question to choose from to answer.

☐ The question and area for answer should be on the same page.

(Continued on the next page)

- Avoid "trick questions," "double negatives" or "mixed messages" on test questions.

- Avoid "trick words," such as always, sometimes, none of the above, all of the above, sometimes, never, mostly, few, etc.

- Avoid wordy questions.

- For fill-in-the-blank questions, do not mark off for spelling. Do provide a word bank, and provide a "trigger" word to get the student started. The length of the line of text should mirror the length of the desired answer. Examples:

There are _____ days in a year.

The first president of the United States was _____.

Thomas Jefferson was the _____ president of the United States.

Note: The blank space should be near the end of the question.

- Grade schoolwork and tests for content, not for spelling, grammar, punctuation or penmanship.

- Do not use open-end questions that can have many answers.

- On tests, do not include vocabulary that has not yet been taught or is unfamiliar to the student.

- Organize test questions so that only one question is being asked at a time.

(Continued on the next page)

- ☐ Design test questions around a given conclusion or fact. Be specific as to what the student is to think about.

- ☐ Design tests that divide information into categories.

- ☐ Provide ample spacing between test questions and ample space, with lined spacing, for answering.

- ☐ Give multiple-choice tests (without double negatives), instead of short-answer or essay tests.

- ☐ Allow marked answers on test copy instead of answer sheet.

- ☐ Limit major core subject testing to one per day.

- ☐ Use only one side of the paper for tests.

- ☐ Provide a private exam room with a test proctor.

- ☐ Provide test times that are preplanned to avoid extemporaneous decisions that negatively impact and stress the student on test days.

- ☐ Teach student test-taking strategies, such as skimming through the test first, choosing which questions to complete first, noting how much time to spend on a question depending on the mark value, using process of elimination for multiple-choice or true-and-false questions and highlighting key or signal words.

- ☐ Return graded assignments and tests within three working days of submission. Dyslexic students need immediate feedback as to how well they're doing. Parents can monitor their child's progress more effectively and help them self correct future assignments.

- ☐ Other: _____

- ☐ Other: _____

(Continued on the next page)

Textbooks and Reading Materials:

- ☐ Teacher-prepared written assignments and materials should be typed, with text size 14 and 1.5 line spacing, avoiding overcrowding of text per page and avoiding multiple fonts.

- ☐ Provide ample spacing of reading materials, between questions and generous amounts of space for answering.

- ☐ Use only one side of the paper for reading assignments.

- ☐ Avoid "overly busy" worksheets that have speech bubbles, diagrams or drawings.

- ☐ Use diagrams and illustrations to break up large sections of text.

- ☐ Use clear, unambiguous pictures with key words or short sentences.

- ☐ Use numbers or bullet points, rather than continuous prose.

- ☐ Check readability of teacher-provided worksheets so that the dyslexic student will be able to read and understand them easily.

- ☐ Provide written outlines and notes of key material.

- ☐ Provide audiobooks of school textbooks and novels. Offer movies, videos and digital media instead of printed versions.

- ☐ Provide an extra set of textbooks for use at home only.

- ☐ Other: _____

- ☐ Other: _____

(Continued on the next page)

Student Organization/Time Management:

- ☐ Teacher will meet with student weekly to develop schedules to study material for future tests, and will assist with prioritizing assignments and class projects.

- ☐ Train the student in basic study habits. Share study tips with the student, including (a) scheduling the most difficult tasks first, when energy is high, (b) breaking larger assignments into smaller, more management chunks, (c) mixing and varying study tasks to avoid monotony, (d) setting clear timelines by establishing how much time is needed to accomplish each step, and (e) using special techniques on how to be flexible with time when unforeseen circumstances require a change in study time.

- ☐ Train the student to ask for assistance. The student should feel comfortable asking for help from the teacher at any time, and not be directed to ask a student for the answer.

- ☐ Create a daily assignment sheet on which the student can record daily homework assignments, which is verified as completed, prior to the end of class (and before the school bell).

- ☐ Provide a formal work plan. In advance of more complex assignments, such as research papers, give the student an outline of a work plan for completing those assignments. The plan breaks a larger assignment into appropriate sub-steps, such as (a) an estimate of the minimum of "seat time" required to complete it, and (b) setting a calendar-date deadline for completion. The teacher is responsible to check in weekly with the student, verifying work that is currently done and providing guidance on future work.

- ☐ Other: _____

- ☐ Other: _____

(Continued on the next page)

Assistive Technology:

☐ Allow use of calculator(s), memory charts, etc.

☐ Provide digital/electronic/audio books for required school textbooks and novel-book reading.

☐ Allow text-to-speech-to-text devices.

☐ Allow computer word processing with talking spellchecker, grammar checker, word prediction while typing, etc.

☐ Allow digital/electronic recorder for classroom and homework purposes.

☐ Allow student to listen to music with earphones during independent work if this allows him/her to improve concentration and increase productivity.

☐ Other: _____

☐ Other: _____

Reading, Reading Fluency, Mathematics and Writing and Spelling Accommodations:

In addition to the above noted accommodations, it is important to incorporate into the IAP, accommodations in the areas of reading, reading fluency, mathematics, and writing and spelling. A list of these accommodations can be found in this book on the following pages.

☐ **Reading:** On page(s) 226 thru 229, there are 24 recommended accommodations for reading. Choose those that will benefit the student and add them to the IAP.

☐ **Reading Fluency:** On page(s) 230, there are 6 recommended accommodations for reading fluency. Choose those that will benefit the student and add them to the IAP.

(Continued on the next page)

- **Mathematics:** On page(s) 232 thru 235, there are 25 recommended accommodations for mathematics. Choose those that will benefit the student and add them to the IAP.

- **Writing and Spelling:** On page(s) 237 thru 239, there are 16 recommended accommodations for writing and spelling. Choose those that will benefit the student and add them to the IAP.

Student Self-Advocacy:

- With parent involvement, explain the supports (accommodations) the student will receive. Provide examples of the types of support, role playing if necessary, including how to ask for schoolwork help or answers to unclear questions and ways to express personal preferences in their learning style. The more the student is involved in understanding how they learn, the more likely accommodations will be used throughout the school years and beyond.

Acknowledged by:

Teacher: _____ Date: _____

Parent: _____Date: _____

Student: _____ Date: _____

"So what do we do? Anything. Something. So long as we don't sit there. If we mess it up, start over. Try something else. If we wait until we've satisfied all the uncertainties, it may be too late"

-Lee Iacocca

Aaron age 13

"The goal of education is the
advancement of knowledge
and the dissemination of truth."

-John F. Kennedy
35th President of the
United States of America

CHAPTER 39

Failure to Identify

Laws that are written to provide a free appropriate public education for our children are only as good as their implementation. Without proper oversight and continuous monitoring of outcomes, things can easily fall through the cracks unnoticed.

The Right to a Free Appropriate Public Education
(FAPE)

A good example of oversight neglect is in the locating and identifying of children suspected of a learning disability. If not located, identified and evaluated, these same children are denied educational support and services that are critical to their academic success. Therefore, failure to identify is a complete violation of the right to a free appropriate public education (FAPE).

School districts are ultimately charged with the responsibility of locating, identifying and evaluating school-aged children, but the districts rely almost completely on teachers, principals and educational support staff to perform this task. If followed correctly, teachers and support staff, are first to notice a problem and refer the student for evaluation. In practice however, many educators fail to identify students with potential learning disabilities, because they lack knowledge and training as to what and how specific learning disabilities, such as dyslexia, affect learning. It's a vicious circle, and the unidentified child suffers the consequences. If there is a violation because the child was never identified, or the child should have been identified earlier and wasn't, the school district might owe compensatory education. Violations of FAPE also include delays in performing special education evaluations/assessments, not following mandated timelines and/or insisting on performing Response to Interventions (RTI) first.

Inappropriate and poorly designed individual education plans (IEPs) can also violate a child's rights to a free appropriate public education (FAPE). An incorrect evaluation and/or diagnosis can impose the wrong educational supports/services (or lack thereof) on an IEP. When this occurs, the student has been denied a FAPE and could therefore be legally entitled to "compensatory" education remedies.

Another example of a FAPE violation is when the classroom teacher and/or special education team fails to implement the IEP appropriately and deviates from the plan as to when services should be provided. Deviations in implementing an IEP are a violation of FAPE and grounds for entitlement to a compensatory education award for the student.

Not providing the IEP services in the right way can also trigger a FAPE violation. If a teacher was improperly trained and delivered or taught a service plan out of sequence or skipped certain vital instructional steps, and the students fails to make benchmark goals, then the student has been denied a free appropriate public education.

Compensatory Education Claims

Parents typically file for compensatory education claims when they believe their child has been denied FAPE. A resolution meeting to try to work things out is usually exhausted prior to moving onto mediation or a due-process hearing. The mediation option is available only if both parties want it; otherwise, the due-process hearing is the next step. A hearing officer will consider all evidence and testimony and issue a decision, awarding or denying compensatory education. An award will specify the nature and amount of compensatory education.

Compensatory education rewards can be in the form of additional education supports and services (typically over and above services provided in the IEP), and/or money. Awards of additional education services are in the form of "hours," either of a particular service or as a "bank" of hours that can be drawn from, for a variety of services. Sometimes banked hours are converted, by agreement, into an actual dollar amount (total value), which can be used for additional services within or outside the school district.

Loosely monitored "Child Find" obligations, improperly trained school and teaching staff, and/or ignoring the law, ultimately results in violating our children's rights to the free appropriate public education that they deserve.

"One test of the correctness of educational procedure is the happiness of the child."

-Maria Montessori
Italian Physician and Educator

CHAPTER 40

Evaluation Report and Supporting Documentation for the IEP Meeting

A major component of a student evaluation for possible learning disability is the school psychologist assessment report. A thorough evaluation should include the following tests and sub-tests:

Tests:

- Verbal Comprehension—measures verbal concept formation, verbal reasoning, and knowledge acquired from one's environment.

- Perceptual Reasoning—measures ability to recognize and organize visual stimuli.

- Working Memory—measures how long information is held for use and its effective (or ineffective) result.

- Processing Speed—measures the duration of "thinking time" required to process information.

- Reading

- Mathematics

- Written Language

- Oral Language

Sub-Tests:

- Word Reading—measures accurate and automatic word recognition, letter identification, and letter-sound awareness.

- Reading Comprehension—measures literal (matter-of-fact) comprehension, lexical (relating to vocabulary) comprehension, reading rate, oral reading accuracy/fluency/comprehension and word recognition.

- Pseudo-Word Decoding—measures phonological decoding (sounds given to language) and accuracy of word attack (decoding, pronouncing and understanding unfamiliar words).

- Numerical Operations—measures counting, numerical identification and writing and calculations (addition, subtraction, multiplication, division, fractions and decimals).

- Math Reasoning—measures multi-step problem solving, money, time, measurement, geometry, reading and interpreting charges and graphs, statistics and probability, estimation and identifying patterns.

- Spelling—measures sound-letter awareness, written spelling of regular and irregular words and written spelling of homonyms (combining spelling and comprehension).

- Written Expression—measures organization, vocabulary, theme development (underlying idea of a story) and such mechanics as spelling and punctuation.

- Listening Comprehension—measures receptive vocabulary (understanding vocabulary when used by others), expressive vocabulary (using vocabulary in conversation) and listening-inferential comprehension (listening to something and mistakenly inferring something else instead).

- Oral Expression—measures oral word fluency, auditory short-term recall of content, story generation, giving directions and explaining steps in sequential tasks. (Order of events or instructions).

Scoring

Evaluation results are then scored and placed into classifications. Below is an example of a Standard Score Reference Chart:

Standard Score	Classification
69 and below	Deficient
70–79	Borderline Deficient
80–89	Below Average
90–114	Average
115–129	Above Average
130 and above	Superior

The standard score(s), along with percentile rank, mental age and grade equivalent, are usually included in the school psychologist evaluation report.

Example for Reading Comprehension

Standard Score: 65 (Deficient)

Percentile Rank: 10% (student scored higher on the test, than 10 of the100 students who also took the same test)

Mental Age: 6:0 (6 years)

Grade Equivalent: <1:0 (less than grade 1)

Gathering Documentation for the IEP Meeting

After the school psychologist evaluation and assessment have been performed, the following documentation is gathered in preparation of the IEP meeting:

1. School psychologist evaluation report.

2. Classroom teacher(s) observations. Parent(s) should request the classroom teacher(s) complete the Teacher Observations forms in this book. These forms (9 areas) are more specific and relevant to students suspected of having dyslexia. Because of their simplicity, teacher(s) should have no problem completing them. The teacher(s) should provide the parent(s) with these completed forms prior to the IEP meeting. Copies should be submitted to the IEP coordinator prior to the meeting.

3. Parent(s) observations. Parent(s) should complete the Parent Observations form(s) in this book that are specific to their child's age (and all prior years, beginning with Early Childhood) and submit them to the IEP coordinator prior to the meeting.

4. Student schoolwork samples. In addition to work samples that will be provided by the classroom teacher(s), parent(s) should also include work samples sent home. Often, teacher-gathered samples of student work do not tell the full story of the student's academic strengths and weaknesses.

5. Student "classroom" observations. This is a report issued by a school team member, other than the student's general education teacher(s), who has observed the student's academic performance in the general classroom setting.

6. Student grades (report card).

7. Student, school standardized test results.

8. Attendance record. If the student has missed school due to being bullied, parent(s) need to annotate the attendance record accordingly.

9. Written report(s) of teacher(s)-implemented academic interventions already provided to the student. Parent(s) should request a copy of these reports prior to the IEP meeting.

10. Independent professional educational evaluation and assessment report(s), if any. These are report(s) provided by parent(s) who have had their child evaluated by an independent clinical/pediatric neuropsychologist or other medical professional.

11. Medical history and/or evaluations, as required.

12. Written recommendations from the School Counselor.

Parent(s) should request, in writing, copies of the above-noted school reports prior to the IEP meeting. In doing so, parent(s) then have time to review the documentation, makes notes and list any questions they may have. Parent(s) should utilize the forms offered in this book (Parent Observations and Individual Accommodation Plan) as a guide.

Note: All forms, in 8½" by 11" (letter size), are available with ownership (purchase) of *A Child's Touchstone*. Go to www.achildstouchstone.com to download them for your use.

Prior to the IEP meeting, parent(s) should organize and place all documentation in a three-ring binder and remember to bring *A Child's Touchstone* to the IEP meeting, using it as a guide as needed.

Sybil age 14

"What sunshine is to flowers,
smiles are to humanity."

-Mary Ann Evans
English Journalist
(aka pen name, George Eliot)

CHAPTER 41

Learning a Foreign Language

From our very first breaths, we're immersed in learning a language we do not yet speak. Our parents lovingly walk and talk us through activities using movement and emotion, which is intimately tied to learning a language. Over time, we're introduced to new patterns, sounds and symbols while learning to read and write.

Learning a second language is not as naturally occurring as one's native tongue. Most often, second-language learning occurs inside a classroom. Students learn using typical grammar and syntax rules of the language, from simple to complex.

Learning a language requires making connections between sounds, what they mean, and how writing represents them. Memory is a crucial part of that process. If you can't remember a sound, the connection is lost. And since children with dyslexia have memory issues, it makes sense that they would also struggle to learn a second language.

Children with dyslexia need an emphasis on developing verbal, rather than written, communications when learning a second language, such as:

- Keeping classes active—allowing moving while learning (less sitting).

- Focusing on listening and moving in response to what the teacher says, such as stand up, walk to the door, open it, close the door, turn around, kiss your left knee, stick your tongue out, smile, whistle, or stamp your foot.

- Teaching only twelve words at a time.

- Teaching gestures that describe each word (by association).

- Having students draw a sketch for each word.

- Having students create an illustrated dictionary.

- Having the illustrated words worked into a mini story that they then act out. The stories should be funny or bizarre on purpose, so they can remember them.

- Having students talk about the funny story in the language being taught. It doesn't matter if what they are saying isn't grammatically correct. The point is to engage the students in dialogue.

- Having students make a craft item that represents the language being taught.

- Having students learn about different types of food typical of the language being taught.

- Having students create a dinner menu (including desert and beverage), describing the food and type of preparation. Place the menu on cardstock and add some artistic flair.

- Incorporating games and songs into language learning.

- Using interactive/on-line digital world language software programs, which can be downloaded onto computers, notepads and other classroom technology devices.

- Slowing down the dialogue. Students need time to process what the teacher is saying. Clear enunciation is also important.

By emphasizing real-life experiences, students are free to generate all kinds of expressions using the language they are learning. Students often do not realize how much they are learning while they are highly engaged. An active (moving) environment in the classroom makes learning more interesting and enjoyable.

Sign Language
as a Second Language

Some students with dyslexia have difficulty learning a second language, especially in the written form. It is very stressful learning another language when a memorization deficit already exists. In this case, dyslexic students may choose to learn sign language.

Sign language is made up of gestures, rather than words, and is a satisfying alternative for the dyslexic learner. The kinesthetic approach used in communicating in sign language is more of a right brained activity. Most children with dyslexia are right brain dominant and therefore find sign language more adaptable to their learning style.

The good news is that more colleges and universities are accepting sign language as meeting the second language requirement.

Language Learners
with Learning Disabilities

No matter where one lives, knowing how to properly speak and write in that country's native language has obvious benefits. Learning a foreign language (second language), however, has its challenges. Toss in grammar rules, dialect or innuendo, and even the most sophisticated language learner can be stumped.

Most countries today represent people of all nations, intertwined with multi-cultural ideals and diverse lifestyles, embodied with many languages.

Children with learning disabilities who also have language-learning issues face additional challenges. Not only do they process information differently, they're also burdened with language barriers that deter or prevent learning.

This is problematic in academic learning environments, when special education services do not match the needs of the student who also requires language learning services. Violations in special education services occur when language learners with learning disabilities are not provided with special education services until language learning improves first, or they are provided special education services without language learning support at the same time. It is only when these services are provided together that learning is most effective.

Laws require that schools provide, to language-learning students with learning disabilities, both language assistance and disability-related services to which they are entitled.

"If a child is to keep alive his inborn sense of wonder without any such gift from the fairies, he needs the companionship of at least one adult who can share it, rediscovering with him the joy, excitement and mystery of the world we live in".

–Rachel Carson,
Marine biologist and conservationist

Bella age 14

"Where words fail, music speaks."

-Hans Christian Anderson
Author of Children's Books and Fairy-tales

CHAPTER 42

Music and the Brain

Without question, the brain loves the sounds of music. Music affects our mood in many positive ways. Music training can also boost everything from pitch perception to visual and motor skills.

Surprisingly, the most pleasant music for the listener's brain is classical music, such Mozart and Beethoven, as well as mid-to-late Baroque composers.

The higher the music pitch, the more positive the effect on the brain. Slower, minor keys warm the brain, which fosters alertness. Faster, major keys cool the brain, which fosters better moods.

Baroque and classical music are beneficial in learning mathematics. This is because mathematics has a sequential method, similar to that in music, and the brain likes it!

Studies show that music training may also improve language processing abilities, similar to learning letters and words through song. In fact, music is a kind of multi-sensory activity that can improve a person's ability to decipher different tones and enhance reading and speech functions.

Music is an amazing tool for teaching almost anything. Music can set a mood, signal a change from one activity to another or help to make a classroom warm and inviting. Teachers can play music to set a certain tone from the start of class. Planning the daily class schedule with musical cues helps students recognize what is happening next.

Children love music repetition (singing the same song over and over), which helps build networks in the brain. Teachers should incorporate music into everyday school activities, encouraging all students to join in. Music invites openness, creativity and fun ways to learn. Research suggests that early interventions based on musical games may offer benefits for learning to read.

Teachers and parents can include music in everyday learning to help children with dyslexia. By using familiar songs, children can hum to themselves while completing homework or taking a test or reminding themselves of the facts or rules they must follow. Even high school and college students can benefit from familiar tunes to remember facts for exams.

Here are some examples:

- Introducing songs from different eras and cultures to help students learn history and social studies.

- Using rhymes or songs to learn grammar.

- Clapping to music to improve understanding of patterns and sequences.

- Clapping to music while breaking words into syllables.

- Listening to lyrics of a song and writing down the words, to help improve listening.

- Spontaneously breaking into dance with uplifting music, in the middle of a classroom lesson.

For those who can remember first grade, music was a part of regular education. Drums, cymbals, triangles, castanets, harmonicas, sticks and sandpaper bars were the instruments, along with the sweet sounds of young children singing. And each year, the instruments changed, as did the types of music played and sung. It was part of every student's regular curriculum, because it was important to learning.

Sadly, many children don't get to experience music like they should. Budgets seem to control what's taught and what isn't, and music and art, for the most part, no longer exist in the school environment. Maybe it's time to bring it back.

Ryan age 14

"I am seeking. I am striving.
I am in it with all my heart."

-Vincent van Gogh
Post-Impressionist Painter

CHAPTER 43

Art Inspired Learning

For many children, expressing themselves through art is their only sanctuary. It's a place where talent and freedom of expression flourish without judgment or criticism.

Children with dyslexia naturally gravitate to expressing their understanding through visual representation. Unfortunately, many educators believe that the only way to measure a student's knowledge is through reading and writing. This is a mistake.

If asked to interpret their knowledge through art, most dyslexic children would go beyond what was required and present a masterpiece of extraordinary understanding.

If teachers and administrators were more open to artistic expression in learning, student expectations would be overflowing with positive results. The classroom would become 3-D and evolve into a place for higher "senses" learning. The kids would be excited to go to school and more engaged in learning everything.

Teachers need to experiment with intuitively good ideas that are different, even if there isn't yet exhaustive research on their innovative teaching methods. And why not? Why wait ten years for a study to be completed, an analysis written and data provided, before trying something new in the classroom? Whose classroom is it anyway? Teachers need to take the lead and use "next practices" as their new mantra.

To get teachers started, here are a few examples of art-inspired learning:

- Create a storyboard. Film and stage directors always create a storyboard before they begin a scene. Students can create their own storyboard by first illustrating and then scripting each board.

- Design a comic book. Students can use their imagination or past experiences to design a comic book with storyline and graphics.

- Expressive writing with pictures from magazines. Students can write a story using pictures and captions.

- Paint, draw, photograph, carve or wood-burn into art, a story. Students get to choose to tell a story in their own art medium, such as carving a piece of wood into a native-Indian totem pole and then describing, in two or three written paragraphs, what its message represents.

- Provide students with a picture or photograph and, through classroom discussion, have them write a short poem that reflects their representation as to its meaning.

- Have students draw a mystical map of a world they envision and then briefly describe how its existence benefits mankind.

- Incorporate art into math lessons by having students create three-dimensional objects.

- Allow students to present a video or PowerPoint presentation in lieu of a written essay.

Teachers need to be free to express their different teaching styles without fear of not following the "check-the-box" rules on everything!

"The most direct and enduring way to reach the mind and imagination of the learner is through the mind, imagination and character of the outstanding teacher."

- Lowell Milken, Co-founder
of Knowledge Universe

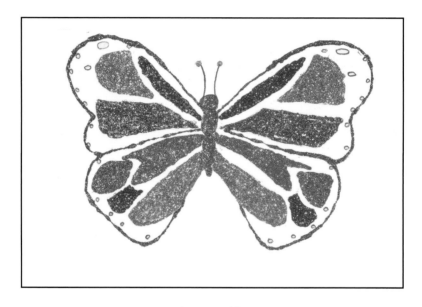

Ivy age 11

"Just when the caterpillar thought the world was over, it became a butterfly."

-Proverb

CHAPTER 44

Stress, Fear and Anxiety

We know that stress can activate all kinds of negative physical and emotional responses. For dyslexic children, daily struggles with educational demands beyond their control result in dramatic rises in emotions and stress levels that severely deter their ability to think clearly.

When stressed, dyslexic children become overwhelmed and lost, not knowing where or how to begin. They are embarrassed and sad, desperate to escape to somewhere quiet. They shut down.

A negative spiral of failure continues. Fears intensify, making even simple tasks, such as talking (without stuttering) and/or daily schoolwork, more difficult. They may shake or tap their feet frantically, deliberately distract themselves by redirecting their eyes and attention elsewhere, nervously chuckle, or put their head down and stay silent. It's no wonder why dyslexic children withdraw and isolate.

A dyslexic's physical being is also affected. Hair loss, weight loss, headaches, mental fatigue, fear of confrontation and avoidance from others are also prevalent.

Some suggest these students are easily distracted because they lack motivation and attention. However, they aren't considering the underlying causes at work. The student's brain is actually working five to fifteen times harder than that of a non-dyslexic; desperately trying to process the information but unable to keep up.

Dyslexic children need our help, patience and understanding.

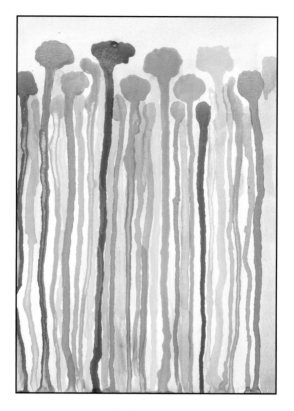

Alicia age 8

"A child's life is like a piece of paper on which every passer by leaves a mark."

-Proverb

CHAPTER 45

Reducing School Stress

Dyslexic student in constant state of fear of criticism by teachers or peers cannot learn. Knowing this, teachers must set the tone in the classroom and defuse any anxiety. Accomplishing this requires the teacher to:

- Never allow other students to correct the dyslexic student's assignments or tests.

- Never distribute or collect tests or homework by passing papers down the row, where other students could see the dyslexic's corrected handwriting, spelling and/or mistakes.

- Never call upon the dyslexic student to read aloud, without getting their permission in advance and giving them a chance to practice the passage.

- Never force the dyslexic to come to the front of the class and write on the board, where other students can critique spelling mistakes and struggling handwriting skills.

- Never force the dyslexic to compete in academic competitions without their permission in advance and offering to help them practice, even during off school hours.

- Never allow other students in the classroom to tease or laugh at the dyslexic student. To do so gives permission for that negative behavior to continue.

- Never ignore or disregard a dyslexic student's silent behavior. Instead, approach the student with gentle concern and help them through the moment.

- Never show frustration towards the dyslexic student. Frustration indicates ignorance and a lack of knowledge and understanding.

- Never tell the dyslexic student they should talk to other students about any questions on assignment work. Such instruction tells the student that the teacher doesn't have time for them.

- Never dismiss the dyslexic student's concerns of being taunted, teased or called names during class that went unnoticed by the teacher. Such dismissal indicates to the student that the teacher is not concerned or interested in helping them.

- Never tell the dyslexic student that teachers are not required to teach differently to them. Professional educators are capable of teaching differently to all students—they simply need to choose to do so.

- Never tell the dyslexic student that they are receiving academic support and it's unfair to other students.

- Never dismiss dyslexia as a student crutch. Such a comment shows ignorance.

- Never give up on the dyslexic student.

- Never stop learning everything possible about dyslexia in order to help the dyslexic student.

If teachers follow these promises, dyslexic student stress in the classroom will be dramatically reduced.

"The secret in education lies in respecting the student."

- Ralph Waldo Emerson (1803-1882),
American poet and lecturer

Jack age 9

"I miss going to bed with absolutely nothing on my mind."

-Anonymous

CHAPTER 46

Reducing Stress at Home

It is important that the entire family be committed to helping the dyslexic child diffuse daily stress. This includes visiting family and friends. Everyone should have a reasonable understanding of how dyslexia affects the child and how they can help.

Here are some suggestions:

- Re-organize their bedroom. Repaint the walls a soft color (but not white). Replace their bedding and window coverings with complementing colors, but avoid bold colors or wild themes. Think calm and comfortable. Re-organize their bedroom, closet, dresser drawers, toy box, etc., and replace old containers with new ones. The goal is to eliminate visual clutter around them as much as possible.

- Remove all electronic devices from their bedroom. This includes the phone, computer, notepad, tablet, etc. They may not like this, but it's important they don't isolate to their rooms. Socialization and family time are paramount. Move the computer to a central location so that the child is still interacting and present at all times with the rest of the family.

- Choose a place for homework. The dining room table can work well, so long as it is clear of clutter, it has proper lighting and the child's school books and supplies are easily accessible. Homework habits need consistency, free of distraction. This is a time when everyone needs to quiet the noise and allow the dyslexic student to do their homework. It is also important that at least one adult family member be close by to answer questions, encourage staying on task, and offer help as needed. Providing a light snack or "chill time" before starting homework can help reduce stress and engage learning.

- Focus homework success on what the dyslexic student is able to complete. It's okay if only half the homework gets done. A parent can always ask the teacher to give the child more time to complete it.

- A dyslexic child will forget things and make mistakes. Let them know that they can make mistakes and still be loved. It's not the child's fault that they forget things—they can't help it. In time and with the family's help and patience, the dyslexic child will learn strategies and tools that will help support them.

- Place all school work in one binder, organized into subjects or tasks. Loose papers always seem to get misplaced if not hole punched and placed in the binder each day. Help the student keep their binder organized daily, and this will help reduce stress.

- Allow time for family time. Play games that encourage family participation. Children with dyslexia love chess, which helps with focus and learning strategy techniques. Board games, card playing and word games are also excellent brain exercises.

- Exercise of any kind reduces stress. Go for a family walk after dinner. Play a game of tag. Grab a basketball or soccer ball and kick it around. Get the dyslexic child involved in a sport group activity or team. Get them moving.

- Break down tasks for the dyslexic child by writing them down. Numbering them in order is also helpful. Describe each task in detail and in proper order. For example—instructing to "put dinner dishes in dishwasher" is fine, but if the dishwasher needs emptying, this is stated first. This may seem tedious, but it is necessary.

- Hobbies are excellent self-rewarding stress relievers. Arts and crafts, drawing, painting, models and block building, clay works, beading, knitting or sewing can give hours of enjoyment and be very calming and self-satisfying for the dyslexic child.

- One of the best ways to engage a dyslexic child in reading is to have them read to the family pet. A dog, cat or bird is a great reading companion. Studies show that pets have a very calming effect on humans. Pets are non-judgmental and love unconditionally. They love attention, and reading to a pet seems to interest both pet and reader. For added interest, there are book publishers that will personalize the storyline to your child, creating characters that are named after pets, family members and friends.

- Children with dyslexia can only do one thing at a time. There is no such thing as multi-tasking for the dyslexic. If not noted, they will forget the task. If there are too many tasks to complete, they may become exhausted and give up altogether, even before starting. In other words, giving a dyslexic a 500-page novel to read will only discourage them from starting—versus a short story they can conquer and feel good about.

- Learn to pause and stay calm during frustration with the dyslexic child. It's not their fault they can't get things done the same way as their siblings. It's not their fault their brain receives and processes information differently than everyone else's. It isn't their fault they need extra patience and understanding from those closest to them.

Jewel age 16

"Shame is the lie someone
told you about yourself."

-Anais Nin
French Author

CHAPTER 47

Feelings of Shame

Shame is usually associated with invalidation by others and refers to a failure to treat a person in a way that conveys attention, respect and understanding.

Dyslexic children that are "shame motivated" by their teachers and parents suffer serious side effects. Their learning reverses into a downward spiral of dangerous shameful feelings that they are unable to manage or cope with.

None of us like to engage in activities that cause us to feel ashamed, and yet we think it's somehow okay to tell a dyslexic child that their learning difference is a problem.

For the dyslexic child, constantly being told to "just try harder" (because it's really seen as the child's issue) translates into, "There's no hope for me because I can't do what everyone is asking of me."

Dyslexic children that endure daily emotional feelings of shame and unworthiness may resort to ending their pain by slowly disconnecting from family, friends and school, abusing drugs or alcohol, cutting themselves or even committing suicide.

Shame on those who believe the dyslexic child is in full control of their academic abilities and motivation to learn! No child is capable of managing their academic challenges without parental and teacher support. Those who believe that a child with dyslexia is using their disability as a crutch, is choosing to be lazy, doesn't care about their homework, seems deliberately bored and disengaged in class, and is not interested in learning—simply lack knowledgeable training and understanding on school-aged children with dyslexia.

In order to counteract the shameful behavior of others, the dyslexic student needs to learn resiliency early in life, and not allow the negative feedback from others to define them.

Failure is not uncommon, which is why resiliency is so important. Knowing that you can simply "go around" a negative person or comment empowers the mind to keep going forward, no matter what others may think or believe.

Dyslexia is not a dirty word that is whispered to parents during an evaluation.

It's important for parents to be honest and forthcoming when discussing dyslexia with their child. It may actually be a relief to the child to know he/she is not stupid or slow or lazy and that all those negative comments are untrue. Disclosure and honesty can offer new beginnings, active plans for support, and a renewal of hope and understanding that previously did not exist.

Turn shame of dyslexia into owning it! Welcome them to the club, because mostly likely, a parent or close family member also has dyslexia. In reality, they're part of a very special community of very creative, fun-loving people.

"Rebellion against your handicaps get you nowhere. Self-pity gets you nowhere. One must have the adventurous daring to accept oneself as a bundle of possibilities and undertake the most interesting game in the world - making the most of one's best."

- Harry Emerson Fosdick, American pastor

Avery age 11

"My best friend is the one who brings out the best in me."

-Henry Ford
Founder of the Ford Motor Company

CHAPTER 48

Self-Esteem

We are not born with self-esteem. It is a gift given to us by our parents, our loved ones, our teachers and mentors, our experience of time and our gratefulness of others. Without self-esteem, we are not complete and stay lost in the shadows of true living.

Dyslexic children who are seen by teachers and targeted by peers as being academically different, face enormous challenges in overcoming that stigma. Schoolwork is red marked and poor grades are annotated without a second thought, and the student is left to suffer consequences they do not deserve and cannot defend.

And because their self-esteem is emotionally damaged by negative feedback, they're more vulnerable to failure and susceptible to all kinds of abuse.

In order to protect themselves, the dyslexic child begins hiding a disability they don't even know they have. Schoolwork goes missing, test results never make it home, and graded homework disappears. This is the only way the dyslexic child can cope with the pain of failure and continued emotional torture. Negative comments from teachers strike deep, and the dyslexic student begins shutting down by creating compensating strategies to block their pain. Becoming emotionally numb becomes a safe place.

When a child loses their self-esteem, they feel they're stupid and become filled with self-limiting beliefs. They begin to shut down and give up—on everything. This is a very dangerous place for a child.

Unless parents and teachers become knowledgeable on dyslexia and how it affects learning, children with dyslexia will continue to suffer.

Children are like puppies. They rely completely on others for support and protection. Be that "rock"—strong, supportive and encouraging. Never give up on them, no matter what. Comfort them when they hurt—tell them everything will be all right because you are there to make that happen. Tell them that no matter what mean things others say, it's not true, because you know them best. Focus on their passions, strengths and talents. Listen to them and their feelings, while cuddling them in your arms. Tell them you love them, shower them with hugs and kisses, and then go get ice cream. Repeat again tomorrow.

"Your time is limited, so don't waste it living someone else's life. Don't be trapped by dogma - which is living with the results of other people's thinking. Don't let the noise of others opinions drown out your own inner voice. And most important, have the courage to follow your heart and intuition. They somehow already know what you truly want to become. Everything else is secondary."

-Steve Jobs (1955 - 2011),
Co-founder of Apple Inc.

Elias age 8

"Nobody rises to low expectations."

-Calvin Lloyd

CHAPTER 49

Low Expectations

Children begin school full of curiosity and eagerness to learn. They can become quickly disillusioned, however, if their academic experience turns into unexpected failure due to an unidentified learning disability.

Parents and educators often misinterpret the unidentified dyslexic child's seeming lack of motivation as laziness and disinterest in learning, that somehow the child has made a conscious effort to choose this direction. Others may equate weakness in basic skills with some sort of inability to think.

A child does not choose laziness, non motivation, and disinterest in learning. It is practically impossible for a child to lack curiosity while observing a ladybug on a leaf, a cocooned caterpillar morphing into a butterfly or a spider building a web. To suggest that some children are naturally lazy or unmotivated is ridiculous.

A child's curiosity is as natural as breathing. And yet some parents and teachers predetermine a child's destiny by identifying them into one of two categories—"I expect them to do well" and "I don't expect them to do well."

The "I expect them to do well" children get treated more positively. With low expectancy, "I don't expect them to do well" students, teachers tend to make less eye contact, smile less, make less physical contact and engage in less playful or light dialogue. Teachers tend to call on low expectancy students less often, ask less challenging questions and reward them less for rigorous responses. Similar to a drama class, the teacher is the director and determines the role of each student. Over time, these students believe and accept their predetermined roles as less capable and unworthy of attention.

Most schools and teachers claim to hold high expectations for all students, even when "expectation favoritism" is obvious and regularly practiced.

Students tend to internalize the beliefs teachers have about their ability. They can rise or fall to the level of their teacher(s)' expectations. Teachers' expectations for students, whether high or low, can become a self-fulfilling prophecy. Students tend to give their teachers "as much" or "as little" of what is definably expected of them.

Studies show that a student's brain responds differently to mistakes made, depending on how authority figures react. A negative remark (such as "stupid" or "lazy") sends signals to the brain that they're expected to do poorly. Over time, the brain shows no sign of surprise or expectation and accepts ridicule of mistakes as gospel.

The brain of a student who doesn't expect good results will eventually fail to learn from mistakes and is destined to repeat them. Simply put, low expectations alter performance and actions and ultimately affect the future.

Schools and teachers that have high expectations for all students and view intelligence as dynamic and fluid, rather than static and unchanging, create a better and happier climate. Caring relationships between teachers and students is also vital to the high-expectation message and its success.

Positive school climate is of utmost importance. If one teacher shows low expectations for one student, the entire school's message has been compromised.

"A friend is one that knows you as you are, understands where you have been, accepts what you have become, and still, gently allows you to grow."

-William Shakespeare,
English playwright

Krista age 13

"Everybody is a genius. But if you judge a fish by its ability to a climb a tree, it will live its whole life believing that it is stupid."

-Albert Einstein
Physicist

CHAPTER 50

Learned Helplessness

Learned helplessness is a taught or conditioned response to certain events. It is not a moral choice. Children in this condition get robbed of independent thought. They're conditioned to believe failure is inevitable, that they're stupid or lack talent.

If the dyslexic child is suffering from depression, learned helplessness will further damage their self-esteem, causing them to fully rely on others for help. The child believes he/she has no control over the learning process, and this belief is confirmed by many failures. Eventually the child gives up trying because it hurts too much.

For example, "one way" learning, taught by one-way teaching, is a form of learned helplessness, because it does not welcome other acceptable ways of learning that contradict the answer. It requires a conditioned response, decided by others.

A dyslexic child influenced with a conditioned response, is first to turn off or give up after failure. Their thinking process stops. They are emotionally unable to counteract the effects of their demise. They believe their failure is permanent.

Permanent expectation of failure creates their helplessness symptoms and may also cause devastating emotional damage.

By third grade, most children have either an optimistic or pessimistic way of seeing the world. Their way of thinking gets shaped by parents, teachers and other adults. Positive output or input results in optimistic children. Negative output or input results in pessimistic children, shaped by criticism from adults who are closest to them, such as parents and teachers. For example, what goes on at school has an effect upon the child, whether positive or negative, because there is no neutral reaction (third option) available.

If a child's learning experiences at school are predominantly negative, they are in danger of becoming depressed. Depression, learned helplessness and negative learned behavior negatively influence the learning process; and this can prevent a child from fulfilling his or her potential. If gone unidentified or ignored, learned helpless children see failure in their ability and in everything they do—in school, sports and home life—as permanent, altering their ability to see themselves as functional and successful beings. Permanent expectation of failure creates helplessness that can last a lifetime.

When children are offered different opportunities to succeed or they have other activities as options for learning, they are happier and healthier. Positive messaging and perception of ability from teachers and parents has the most influence on a child's effort and wellbeing.

Teaching children to reject negative input from others and dispute them will help change their inner dialogue. They can begin empowering themselves by being in control of their own thoughts, and realize that negativity from others does not define them, their effort or their ability.

"This is my wish for you: Comfort on difficult days, smiles when sadness intrudes, rainbows to follow the clouds, laughter to kiss your lips, sunsets to warm your heart, hugs when spirits sag, beauty for your eyes to see, friendship to brighten your being, faith so that you can believe, confidence for when you doubt, courage to know yourself, patience to accept the truth. Love to complete your life."

-David Harkins,
British poet

Lucas age 15

"Sometimes, difficult things need to be said. Don't let discomfort silence you."

-Anonymous

CHAPTER 51

Consequences of Doing Nothing

Within the judicial system, it is a well-known fact that there is a disproportionately high rate of incarcerated juveniles identified as having learning disabilities. A significant percentage are also described as "under-educated", with excessively low literacy skills.

Government funding decisions for the building of more juvenile detention centers often include data gathered from public schools on third through sixth grade student behavior records. It is suggested that students identified with "behavioral markers" (lacking school effort) are less likely to complete high school, and/or more likely to end up in prison.

Hence, decisions of doing nothing or not enough to help children with dyslexia, has serious consequences. Dyslexic children that go un-assessed, undiagnosed and untreated can become statistics of a lifetime nightmare. Their suffering is real and comes in the following forms:

- High School Drop-out – A shocking eighty-five percent of school drop-outs are children with learning disabilities that have not been identified, and most are dyslexic. This silent epidemic is the precursor of the school-to-prison pipeline.

- Addiction - Substance abuse (illegal and prescribed drugs), alcohol abuse, cigarette smoking, excessive computer gaming and internet use, and under-age sexual encounters.

Drug abusers are ten times more likely to suffer from dyslexia and represent more than forty percent of the overall drug use by total population.

- Juvenile Delinquency – 85% percent of all juvenile offenders have learning disabilities, such as dyslexia, and get arrested within three to five years of dropping out of high school.

- Repeat Crime Offenders – If no help is given to the suffering dyslexic, it can lead to a life of crime. School failure is highly correlated with criminality.

- Incarceration (Prison) – More than 50% percent of imprisoned inmates have dyslexia. Our children get warehoused in juvenile detention centers, desperately calling for help when no one is really listening. Repeat offenses are high among children who don't get appropriate academic and family support.

- Throwaways/Runaways and Homelessness – Some parents give up on their troubled child and throw them out of the house. Child abandonment has risen dramatically, as has children running away from home. The suffering child ends up on the streets and homeless.

- Poverty and Health Issues – Undiagnosed and untreated dyslexic adults sometimes cannot properly care for themselves, which can lead to poverty, malnutrition and serious health issues.

- Unemployable and Requiring Social Assistance – Suffering dyslexics may have difficulty acquiring and keeping a job. They lack academic and coping skills, which reduce opportunities for advancement.

- Loss of Overall Quality of Life – If left undiagnosed and untreated, the dyslexic's overall quality of life is deeply undermined. Inadequate educational instruction and guidance, reduced employment opportunities, jeopardized health, family neglect and isolation are typical life drainers.

- Death - For some children with dyslexia, the suffering is just too painful and they choose to commit suicide. Suicide among our youth has dramatically increased, as has the ways in which they take their lives.

Decisions to do nothing are usually based on ignorance of adults that are custodians of the dyslexic child. This may include parents, teachers, principals, administrative educators and medical professionals.

It's not the dyslexic child's fault if they end up in a juvenile detention facility. It's not their responsibility to diagnose their learning disability or figure how to help themselves. It is up to the adults closest to the dyslexic child, to locate, identify, assess, diagnose and offer academic support as soon as possible. If these same adults lack knowledge and information due to misinformation or ignorance, there's no blaming the dyslexic child. After all, they're just children and rely on adults closest to them to guide their lives.

Decisions to do nothing are usually based on ignorance of adults who are custodians of the dyslexic child. These may include parents, teachers, principals, administrative educators and medical professionals.

It's not the dyslexic child's fault if they end up in a juvenile detention facility. It's not their responsibility to diagnose their learning disability or figure how to help themselves. It is up to the adults closest to the dyslexic child to locate, identify, assess, diagnose and offer academic support as soon as possible. If these same adults lack knowledge and information due to misinformation or ignorance, the dyslexic child is not to blame. After all, they're just children, and they rely on adults closest to them to guide their lives.

Alexandra age 10

"Our lives begin to end the day we become silent about things that matter."

-Martin Luther King Jr.
American Pastor and Civil Rights Leader

CHAPTER 52

Ignorance

There is an alarming lack of knowledge by parents and educators about dyslexia. Children with dyslexia face daily uneducated and hurtful remarks, and no one seems to realize the emotional damage that is taking place. It's called ignorance.

There are three types of ignorance regarding dyslexia:

- The first type of ignorance of dyslexia is the uninformed. The uninformed represent 70% of the population. This doesn't mean they're uncaring, it just means that their lives are not affected or associated with dyslexia and its symptoms. And in most cases, they're unaware of anyone closest to them— family, friends, relatives, loved ones, colleagues or associates— struggling from dyslexia.

- The second type of ignorance of dyslexia is the misinformed. The misinformed usually rely on their knowledge from what they've heard from others, who are also misinformed. This could be problematic when the misinformed are ignorant of dyslexia and are in positions where learning disabilities are in the forefront, such as in school environments. These misinformed types tend to believe they are more knowledgeable about learning disabilities than the average uninformed person and exert authority when in their presence. For the most part, they go unquestioned or unchallenged regarding their knowledge of dyslexia, empowering them to impose their erroneous views and opinions as gospel.

- The third type of ignorance of dyslexia are those with knowledge who remain willfully ignorant by choice. Also known as "willful blindness," the willfully ignorant choose to behave with ignorance, refusing to change, standing firm on their "I don't want to deal with this" attitude and denying the dyslexic child any help from them. These willful characters are found in every profession. Sadly, our educational system is not immune to this type of ignorance, which can create a toxic learning environment for children with dyslexia.

Ignorance can sometimes breed contempt and spread quickly. A shocking number of educators and school administrators still believe that learning disabilities occur in children because of their home environment.

For decades, educators have enforced "reading to learn" policies, even though 40% of students do not learn that way. However, no matter the "reading to learn" enforcement, children with dyslexia will never successfully learn to their full potential unless educators agree to teach how these children learn (not the other way around).

One of the best ways to counter ignorance about learning disabilities is to educate. This book does just that!

"Learn from yesterday, live for today, hope for tomorrow. The important thing is not to stop questioning."

-Albert Einstein,
Physicist

Jeremy age 15

"Let no one ever come to you without leaving better and happier."

-Mother Theresa

CHAPTER 53

Bullying and Disability Harassment

Children have the right to be loved unconditionally, nurtured abundantly and protected valiantly—to have their feelings respected and nurtured in ways that allow them to develop a sense of self-worth. They also deserve a safe environment, free of intimidation, while under the care of their school.

Bullies typically demand high social standing among their classmates. If someone questions their authority, they too can become the bullied. Bullies believe they are physically and psychologically stronger than those they choose to associate with. They consider themselves tough, dominant and "cooler" than everyone else. They prefer to seek passive (those who seem quiet, timid and non-confrontational) or proactive (those who challenge them, or are less intimidated), as bullying targets. The goal is to invoke fear and superiority over those they don't like.

Most schools have a zero tolerance policy when it comes to bullying, but ultimately that is not enough if the administration turns a blind eye to the situation. It isn't enough to retroactively discipline bullies long after the bullying has taken place. School administration needs to get involved early and often. This is especially true if the bullying is due to a child's disability. One of the largest groups of children who are bullied in school are those with disabilities.

Schools, administrators, teachers and parents should be aware that:

- Bullied children do not feel safe. Imagine waking every morning fearful that the bullying will begin again, and feeling powerless to do anything about it.

- No child causes bullying. Quite often however, bullied children feel it is their fault and that they are failures, unworthy of anyone's help.

- If a child's cry for help from bullying goes ignored, the bullied child will begin to feel invisible, as if he or she doesn't exist. Such ignored victims of bullying begin feeling like non-entities, denying their own needs and protecting themselves from constant emotional pain. They learn to set limits on how much to give others and isolate, because their feelings no longer matter.

- Children with dyslexia are two times more likely to become victims of bullying by their peers and are least likely to receive others' protection from the perpetrators.

- Children with dyslexia are both uniquely vulnerable and disproportionately impacted by the bullying phenomenon.

- Teachers and administrators often dismiss victims' cries for help, claiming that they do not think it necessary to intervene and leaving the children to work it out themselves. Authority figures, teachers and parents, may not recognize certain behaviors as bullying.

- Failing to stop the bullying implies unspoken approval of the behavior. This enables bullies while it condemns victims and bystanders to feel further victimized.

- Dyslexic students will begin to feel physically unsafe on the school playground and emotionally unsafe in the classroom.

Student-on-student (peer-on-peer) bullying can cause serious outcomes to the victim, such as:

- Physical pain—most do not associate physical pain with verbal abuse; however, the brain first "feels" emotional pain. Pain nerves negatively affect the entire physical body.

- Emotional pain—the brain secretes fluids that can feel like burning fuel being injected into the body, causing excruciating emotional pain.

- Depression—bullying is abuse. Abuse can cause chronic depression in dyslexic children. The child's brain is unable to cope with excessive bullying.

- Anxiety—the dyslexic child is fearful of the bully and is extremely nervous when around them. In the classroom, the dyslexic is tense, nervous and afraid of being teased, laughed at or taunted without the teacher's noticing.

- Loss of self-esteem and confidence—dyslexic children are unable to defend themselves when the bully overwhelms them with negative verbal abuse and no one counteracts the abuser's authority.

- Loneliness and alienation—the bully usually has a group of followers who go along with the bullying, in fear of being bullied themselves. The dyslexic student feels rejected and isolated by the bully and the followers. The dyslexic student is left to eat lunch alone and be lonely on the playground.

- Shunning by classmates and teachers—shunning means being part of a community (such as a school classroom, playground or activity) but being deliberately ignored.

- Physical activity is compromised—the dyslexic child loses interest in participating in athletics or any outside activities with school peers, in fear of being deliberately targeted and hurt by bullies.

- Personal-hygiene neglect—personal hygiene becomes less important. Bathing, brushing hair, brushing teeth and interest in staying clean become difficult to manage.

- Reduced academic motivation and aspirations—the dyslexic feels helpless. Things and life in general seem less important. Teachers/parents become frustrated and think the child is not working hard enough in school. The student's grades continue to worsen.

- Reluctance to go to school (absenteeism)—the dyslexic child feels sick, scared, overwhelmed, angry and despondent, is frustrated with teachers and is unwilling to share feelings openly.

- Self-harm and suicidal thinking—bullied children with dyslexia may feel helpless and start thinking of ways to end their pain.

"Bullies do not see the bullied as victims, they see them as prey".

Peer-on-peer bullying of children with dyslexia should never be accepted. Schools are violating the law if they fail to recognize and remedy the misconduct of harassment and bullying, which limit the student's ability to fully benefit from the school's education program. Legal consequences can include civil rights violations when the student misconduct also results in discrimination on the basis of disability (such as dyslexia).

Parents/Family Members Who Bully

Parents and/or family members may not recognize their contribution to bullying the dyslexic child. Parents may compare one child's abilities to that of another, not realizing the damaging effects of their words.

This negative behavior usually occurs when the parents or family members are unaware that the child they are comparing has dyslexia. They see the child as intelligent but yet lacking in so many simple ways. These parents and/or family members have no knowledge of learning disabilities and are ignorant of the consequences.

- The dyslexic child takes abuse from everyone closest to them. Teasing, taunting, ridiculing, insults and degradation are commonplace. Siblings act out towards the dyslexic in a way similar to the behavior of the school bully. The dyslexic child is aware of being treated differently but is unsure why.

- The bullying becomes even more intense when the dyslexic child is also not performing well in school. The parents feel that their child is not working hard enough, is lazy and is in need of academic discipline. This is often confirmed by the child's teachers, who also believe that the student is not living up to potential.

- Dyslexic children are often left believing they are stupid and less worthy because they can't seem to keep up. Parents call them "the runt of the litter," "the slow one" or "the problem child." Teachers call them "the below average student needing improvement."

Teachers Who Bully

It is difficult to conceive or accept that a teacher would bully a student, and yet the data overwhelmingly indicates that teacher bullying is of major concern. And as school administrators are stretched with other obligations, teacher bullying goes unattended, disregarded or ignored. The bullying teacher becomes more empowered, and the dyslexic student is helpless.

Teacher-to-student bullying is similar to peer-on-peer bullying. It is an abuse of power that is usually expressed while other students are present—in the classroom and on the playing field.

Aggressive bullying is when teachers prefer an audience during their bully act, followed by laughter from the victims' classmates. Aggressive bullying by teachers consists of a more assertive and bold approach. Their behavior towards bullied students is outwardly noticeable.

Aggressive bullying includes:

- Openly and in front of peers, ridiculing or demeaning the dyslexic student for lack of effort or performance in their school work.

- Insisting that the dyslexic student is using their disability as a crutch and demanding more effort.

- Refusing to accept completed work that offers different solutions to the answer, for example, insisting on "one way" math solutions.

- Rejecting the dyslexic student's non-conforming efforts, suggesting that they need to work harder at staying to the curriculum.

- Shouting or screaming at the dyslexic student for not completing an assignment.

- Suggesting that the dyslexic student would do better if they were at a remedial or trade school.

- Admitting that they prefer not to work with these types of students and "did not sign up for this."

- Sarcastically questioning how the dyslexic student got this far without cheating.

- Requiring medical documentation to prove that the student is actually dyslexic, even when a formal assessment and diagnosis has already been performed.

- Deliberately sabotaging any efforts made to improve student outcomes and suggesting that the student doesn't need them.

- Influencing other teachers, administrators, principal, etc., that the dyslexic student is just lazy and unmotivated and that the parents are overprotective.

- Insisting that the dyslexic student is intellectually challenged and needs a special school to accommodate the disability.

- Knowingly compromising the dyslexic student's abilities.

- Refusing to teach strategies that would improve student success.

- Justifying their opinions with uneducated, misinformed and ignorant responses.

- Continuing to reject instructions from school administrators that they need to follow the required student plan.

- Showing false concern over the academic success of the dyslexic student.

- Resenting the dyslexic student for learning differently.

- Exhibiting frustration when the dyslexic student "doesn't get it."

- Continuing to stay willfully ignorant of the student's dyslexia.

Other bullying facts:

- Passive-aggressive bullying is when the teacher has a deeper resentment towards the student, the student's parents and/or school administration. Both aggressive and passive aggressive bullying are further described in this chapter.

- Bullying by teachers includes athletic coaches and those who have supervisory control over students.

- Teacher-to-student bullying is deliberate and calculating. Their goal is to instill threats, humiliation, emotional stress and fear. The teacher feels empowered. Teachers who bully feel their abusive conduct is justified to motivate the student.

- Teachers who bully children with dyslexia usually choose them because they see them as easy (or soft) targets. They're chosen because of some perceived difference (learning difference) that the teacher dislikes. Such target selection is discriminatory and, as such, is recognized as a hate crime.

- Children with dyslexia are usually quieter and less likely to challenge inappropriate behavior, especially from an authority figure. Furthermore, students who are victims of teacher bullying often feel trapped, while the abuser is all-powerful. The dyslexic student may feel that filing a complaint could place them at a higher risk of teacher retaliation.

Passive-Aggressive Bullying

Passive-aggressive bullies are subtle in their approach and usually know the victim in a more personal setting; they may be parents, teachers or athletic/sport coaches, for example. Most passive-aggressive bullies have specific identifiable traits:

- They know and regularly interact with their victims.

- They feel comfortable and secure in their authority and are unconcerned with being challenged.

- Others who are close to the bully (the other parent or family member, school principal or administrator) usually downplay any reports of bullying and side with the perpetrator.

- The bully will often accuse the victim of inappropriate behavior towards their schoolmates, that other students are complaining about them and that it is the victim who needs to change. This is often reported and supported by school personnel or family members, even though there is no evidence to support such a claim.

Dyslexic children have no one who believes them. They feel helpless. They begin to socially withdraw. They stop caring for themselves. Instead, they start finding ways to prevent the pain they are experiencing. In some respects, they are slowly dying.

Passive-aggressive bullying, also known as psychological bullying, is also prominent in schools and may include the following:

- Forgetting to include the dyslexic student in group activities and not immediately correcting the problem so that the student is fully included.

- Acknowledging that the dyslexic student is not included in a group activity and suggesting that the student just blend in without an identified spot on the team.

- Not ensuring that the dyslexic student is part of organized group projects. Instead, they're excluded and accused of not participating.

- Ignoring the dyslexic student during class time, even when they know the student needs help.

- Resenting the dyslexic student's need of academic support and feeling it is unfair to the rest of the class.

- Allowing students to laugh or tease the dyslexic student during class or on the playing field.

- Deliberately ignoring signs of bullying by peers.

- Excluding the dyslexic student from participating in academic competitions because they feel the student is not good enough.

- Using clever sarcasm or unkind words.

- Showing false concern for the dyslexic student and an insincere desire to help.

- Having low expectations for the dyslexic student and grading them accordingly.

Scott age 17

"Service to others is the rent you
pay for your room here on Earth."

-Muhammad Ali
Professional Boxer

Athletic Teachers/Sports Coaches Who Bully

Conduct unbecoming of an athletic teacher or sports coach still exists in our schools. Athletic and sport coaches who bully students have often gotten a "pass" in terms of their bad behavior. And some parents believe that in order for their child to excel in sports, the student needs to toughen up to compete.

But these behaviors, if ignored or unquestioned, condone accelerated offenses towards students with disabilities such as dyslexia.

Some athletic teachers/coaches believe they know what's best for students interested in team sports. These types of coaches believe that a winning team is most important and are willing to "cut" players they believe will not help the team win. They believe being cut from a team sport is character building, and the student will try harder next year. And they are less concerned how "cutting" affects the student because they have several other students they can still choose from. Lastly, they believe that all athletic coaches and schools aspire to this same premise. They are wrong.

Team cutting is not an acceptable method of character building in students. The athletic teacher/coach will inevitably choose to cut students they feel are not good enough and who will not challenge their decision. This is because winning is more important than a student who simply wants to play and be part of the school team.

Sometimes athletic teachers/coaches get caught up in the "winning mode" and forget their overall professional responsibility, which is to ensure that all students have equal opportunities to participate in all sports offered by the school. Nowhere in kindergarten through high school education does it state that a student must be an exceptional athlete or have experience to either participate in a specific sport or continue with that sport.

Children with dyslexia are often subjected to discrimination because a coach feels they are not emotionally committed or physically up to par with the rest of the team, or because they do not academically meet the grade point average (GPA) in order to participate.

Sadly, some coaches use methods such as insults and condescending remarks towards students they want off the team, hoping they'll quit on their own. They are literally bullying the student off the team.

Other forms of unacceptable behaviors:

- Telling the student they're cutting the team size and they'll have to compete against other players for a spot, in hopes it discourages them from wanting to try.

- Suggesting that the student is not really committed to the sport.

- Discouraging the student from wanting to work out with the team by insulting or demeaning their efforts.

- During school, pulling the student out of academic classes to reprimand them for not performing well or for being late to practice.

- Threatening the student months in advance that cuts may occur, to encourage the student to drop out.

- Stating that the reason for the cuts is because of school budgets.

- Continuously criticizing the student for being unable to follow instructions to their satisfaction.

- Criticizing and showing no encouragement when the student makes a wrong play or when the other side scores.

- Cutting the dyslexic student from the team and requiring them to take basic physical education instead.

- Dismissing student concerns that they are being bullied or harassed by other players.

- Believing that they feel it necessary to toughen-up the dyslexic student.

- Believing that cutting or rejecting the dyslexic student from the team builds character.

- Believing that children with dyslexia are never discriminated against when it involves team sports.

- Believing that dyslexic student concerns are not applicable in physical education and sports activities.

- Continuing to stay willfully ignorant of dyslexia.

Athletic teachers and sport coaches are not exempt from understanding dyslexia and how a student's physical and emotional well-being can affect learning.

Chapter 37, on accommodations for dyslexics involved in physical activities and team sports, describes the responsibilities of schools and their physical education teachers in providing appropriate access to students with learning disabilities.

Bullied "By Association"

Sometimes when a complaint of bullying gets filed against a teacher/coach or administrator, the accused will go on the offense and respond by broadening their bullying to those supporting the victim (such as the parents). Such strategy is actually "bullying by association."

The goal is to punish parents or guardians for believing the victim. The effects of bullying by association are felt immediately.

Bullying by association includes:

- Not responding to telephone calls, email messages or letters from the parents or guardians of the bullied student.

- Critiquing the student's homework assignments more severely than in the past, or grading the dyslexic's schoolwork more negatively.

- Soliciting alliances from other teachers and school administrators to create an unfriendly environment for the parents or guardians when visiting the school.

- Deliberately excluding or not notifying the parents or guardians of a special school event that involves their child.

- Sabotaging efforts of parents or guardians involved in class projects, such as not providing all the information or changing the schedule without notice, thereby limiting the student's ability to complete the project on time.

- Not allowing the parents or guardians to spend time in the classroom, saying that all parent participation slots are full.

- Sending notes home stating that the student is misbehaving in the classroom, when no issues have occurred by any other teachers or administrators.

- Telling the parents or guardians that pursuing complaints against them will only make matters worse for the student because their charges are lies.

- Neglecting or refusing to comply with the student's Individualized Education Plan.

Keeping a Bullying and Harassment Log

Parents should watch for any signs of bullying and immediately take appropriate action to protect their child.

Keeping a log of the bullying or harassment is also important. The log should include the date, time and place (on the school playground, in the classroom, on the school bus, etc.), the bully's name and the type of bullying or harassment, such as:

- Physical assault—which includes items such as a basketball being thrown at the victim and inflicting pain.

- Verbal assault—verbally threatening (shouting or screaming) physical harm.

- Non verbal threats—the bully discretely motions signs of aggression towards the victim.

- Emotional threats or intimidation—the bully suggests that the victim has no friends, is not invited to any birthday parties, and can't do anything unless the bully says so.

- Social exclusion and isolation—the bully prevents other classmates from associating with the victim. Students (followers) are often afraid of the bully and will avoid the bullied student during lunch break. The bully does not allow the victim to join any group playground activities.

- Extortion—the bully extorts money, personal items, electronics, completed homework, etc., from the victim.

- Taunting, teasing, gossiping, starting rumors, falsifying accusations, calling names and issuing demeaning put downs—the bully enjoys these types of assaults. It is important to provide a full description of the bully's actions.

- Cyber bullying—the use of computer or telecommunications to send messages or images that are embarrassing, slanderous, threatening or intimidating. Includes email, text messaging, social networks and/or chat lines.

The log should also include the names of student witnesses of the bullying. Other supporting details may include photographs of broken or damaged personal items, torn or stained clothing, broken eyeglasses, destruction of school homework (ripped apart, graffiti or written across, water damaged or thrown in the trash).

If the student was physically assaulted, supporting details may include photographs of physical injury, written details of the injury described by a medical professional, plus treatment required, police report filings and written statements from witnesses to the assault.

Communications Log

Parents should also keep a communications log. The log should include the date and time, name and position of the person(s) communicated with regarding the incident. The following questions should be asked and details of the discussion annotated in the communications log:

- How will the child will be immediately protected from future misconduct by the identified bully?

- What steps are being taken to ensure the child feels emotionally and physically safe at school?

- How will the bully's parents be notified regarding their child's misconduct?

- What supporting documentation (proof) will be provided to ensure the bully's parents have been formally notified? (Parents who knowingly ignore their child's misconduct and permit bullying to continue can become personally liable under the "parental liability law.")

- Who is responsible for implementing and enforcing anti-bullying policy at the child's school?

- Will the school be notifying the bully's teacher(s) regarding the misconduct?

- Will the school be notifying the bullied student's teacher(s) that their student was a victim of bullying and identify the perpetrator?

- Will the playground monitors be notified that the child has been bullied by the identified bully student?

- What types of school counseling will be provided to the child in order to assist in their recovery from such bullying abuse?

- What action will the school administration take if the bully perpetrator continues to bully the child?

- What steps can be taken if the school administration fails to stop the misconduct and the bullying continues?

- Since the child has an identified learning disability (dyslexia), will the person(s) responsible for the child's Independent Educational Plan (IEP) or 504 Plan, be notified and involved in protecting the child's civil rights resulting from discriminatory harassment?

Some school principals and administrators won't be prepared to answer these questions and will suggest putting it in writing. Parents should immediately do so, requesting a written response within 10 days. Administrators, principals and teachers are considered to act *in loco parentis* (in place of parents) during school hours and could become professionally and personally liable for the dyslexic student's physical and emotional suffering if they do not act to protect the student.

Although parents may feel uncomfortable pursuing answers to protect their child, doing nothing is worse. Bullied children are at a much higher risk of depression, anxiety and even suicide.

Formal Notice of Bullying and Harassment

A formal notice of bullying and harassment of your child is meant to serve significant and appropriate notice, to those responsible for enforcing and protecting students from bullying and misconduct that results in discriminatory harassment, that violations have occurred; and the notice requires immediate steps to eliminate and to prevent the harassment and hostile environment from recurring.

Appropriate steps to end the bullying and/or harassment may include preventing the harasser from having any contact with the victim, providing counseling to the victim and taking disciplinary action against the harasser/bully.

If the school (a) fails to recognize that a student is being bullied, harassed and/or discriminated against because of their disability, and (b) does not correct or rectify the hostile environment that constitutes discriminatory harassment, then such failure to act subjects the school and those acting on behalf of the school to criminal and civil liability for the tragic outcomes of the bullied student.

The formal notice of bullying and harassment letter should include:

- The name of the person(s) served and the date served.

- A written list of incidents of bullying and/or harassment, itemizing each incident by type and identifying each offense within the Criminal/Penal Code.

- A statement indicating that (a) they owe a duty of care to all students, (b) they are in a position of trust and (c) they are required to prevent bullying and harassment from occurring and to respond appropriately when it does.

- A statement indicating that those who are hereby served are alerted to the potential legal liabilities, both personally and professionally, if the bullying and harassment does not cease immediately.

- A copy of the Bullying and Harassment Log.

- A copy of the Communications Log.

- A request that the recipient sign for receipt of said letter and return to sender within 10 days.

In the majority of cases, the school will respond positively and take the necessary action to stop the misconduct of the bullying student.

If this does not occur within a reasonable period of time, legal action may be necessary to enforce the laws of the land and protect the child.

Sample Legal-Representation Letter Regarding Bullying

Date:

To: District School Board, School Principal and Teacher(s),
and Parent(s) of the Bully(ies)
c/o each address, per addressee

Re: Name of Child/Student, School Attending and Grade

Dear Sir/Madam:

I am writing on behalf of my client, (name of student), attending (name of school). He/she is being discriminated against and repeatedly bullied during school hours by (name student[s] and/or teacher[s]). This is prohibiting him/her from being able to appropriately access academic learning at his/her school.

The (name of school district) receives federal funds for which it contracts to not discriminate. You have the authority to investigate and correct this discrimination. You also have control over the site and personnel where the discrimination occurs.

If you do not investigate and correct the problem, we may claim that you and the district are deliberately indifferent to the discrimination. If you do not stop the bullying and correct the unlawful discrimination, the school district may be liable for damages, as well as those involved for non-compliance.

My client and his/her parent(s) have provided documentation to support their concerns, including prior written and oral communications made to the teacher(s), principal and other education staff members. This document is attached hereto.

Your immediate attention to my client's concerns is paramount. I look forward to receiving a written response regarding the steps taken by you to protect (name of student) and stop the accused bullies from continuing their abusive behavior.

Sincerely, Name of Legal Representative

Tiffani age 8

"We'll be friends forever, won't we, Pooh?"
asked Piglet. "Even longer" Pooh answered.

-A.A. Milne
English Author

CHAPTER 54

Friendship

Children need friends. Family is great (most of the time), but friends provide a connection to the community and the world that is just as important.

For most children, making friends is easy. Move into a new neighborhood and you'll understand what I mean. It's usually the kids that introduce the parents to each other, not the other way around. A lot of adult friendships begin when their kids play together in a sandbox.

When school-age years begin, new child friendships develop in different ways. And although kids still get to play together on the school grounds, most new friendships will be formed "inside" the classroom.

Most parents are surprised to learn that inside the classroom, the teacher plays an important role in developing a child's ability to make new friends. If a student is shy, the teacher can introduce another student with similar interests or talents, or create group activities that involve sharing of ideas or stories that are engaging and fun. When children feel welcomed by their teacher and classmates, they naturally do better in school.

Teachers who do not present a friendly, positive and respectful environment for learning and collaboration between classmates will inevitably witness teasing, laughter and bullying of students by other students. If ignored by the teacher, other students who are not party to the teasing or bullying will cower to their intimidation or join them in an effort to deflect possible retaliation. In this scenario, positive relationship building is non-existent, and the teacher is part of the problem.

Friends are special. Being called someone's friend is an honor. Friendships in school are extremely important. Having no friends at school (at any age) is devastating. No child should have to play alone on the school playground, eat lunch alone, feel lonely and unwelcomed by classmates, or endure emotional isolation or bullying by peers or adults in their care.

In order for children to develop a strong self-worth and build long-lasting relationships, they need adults (parents, family, teachers, etc.) to protect their vulnerabilities and help them develop friendships that will be there for a lifetime.

Below are some ideas in developing lifetime friendships:

- Early interaction with children of similar age. Little kids seem to know how to communicate with each other, even when no one else understands.

- Allow children to have ownership of their toys before having to share them with siblings or other kids. Children naturally share their toys when they first "feel ownership" over them.

- Kids love routine. Be consistent with playtime/socialization time, downtime, sleep time and school/learning time.

- Arrange friend/classmate sleepovers at your home. Have fun activities involving teamwork (such as parents/adults challenging the kids to a game, whodunit mysteries, or crazy science projects, to name a few.

- Volunteer. As a family, decide on volunteering at a community event, or choose a specific cause in which the family participates on a regular basis. (Kids love this.)

- Join a club of family interest that requires regular participation and builds "pay it forward" values.

- Participate in professional sporting events focused on youth interaction.

- Introduce a "buddy bench" program at your child's school. Parents donate money to purchase a park bench—a place where students who want to socialize during recess or lunch can sit or gather, to let other friendly students know they wish to join them in play. An unveiling of the buddy bench, with its purpose, is presented to the entire school so that all students know the bench is available to them.

- Encourage involvement in school clubs. Most schools offer school clubs in which students can voluntarily participate. Research the types of school clubs and encourage your child to join.

- Let your child shine. Support whatever your child feels passionate about doing or obtaining.

- Parents and teachers should encourage participation in the school debate team because they believe the student has great influence, knowledge and insight.

- Encourage your child to participate in a team sport, even if it involves competing for a particular team position with another schoolmate.

- Build trust on outings. Encourage safe, group-date friendships and outings among teenagers, without parental escort.

- Regularly participate in friend and family gatherings that involve connection, celebration and community involvement.

- Make sure your child knows the truth of the statement, "If you have one or two best friends, you are truly blessed."

Derek age 13

"You can get all A's and still flunk life."

-Walker Percy
American Author

CHAPTER 55

School Isn't Everything

With so much emphasis placed on children academically, it's difficult to see the child through the textbooks. Our little darlings are being smothered by education overload, driven by the desires of well-intentioned parents and educators.

In fact, school isn't everything. It isn't the end of the world if a child misses a few days of school, doesn't get an "A" on every assignment or test, or learns differently from other kids. The most important thing is to have a positive educational experience.

It's a mistake to assume a positive educational experience is only associated with high grades, and a negative educational experience with low grades. An "A" student can be stressed and miserable, while a struggling, barely-getting-C's student can love school. The magic is in the balance.

A love of lifelong learning has very little to do with grades. Constantly nagging children about their schoolwork can backfire. Micro-managing their every waking moment with activities that require constant adult supervision is a recipe for a flat soufflé.

Children often struggle with identity issues, in part because parents mistakenly believe they are responsible for molding their children's identities and try to control the outcomes.

School overload occurs when children become so overwhelmed with trying to manage the academic to-do list that they burn out. Children with dyslexia have it even worse because others believe they're burned out because they are lazy and unmotivated.

Below are some ideas to balance school importance with identity value:

- Play hooky with your kids (but call it a mental health day). Surprise them with something fun to do, like going to the beach, amusement park, snow or water park, bowling, the movies, etc. Be organized, yet spontaneous. Your kids will love the idea and remember the day.

- Enact "schoolwork free" weekends. Adults have two days off from work each week. So should kids.

- School meltdowns and frustration are okay. It's how parent(s) respond that matters. Stay calm, acknowledge their feelings and offer ideas to reduce their anxiety. Telling them to get over it and move on won't work.

- Once in a while, side with your child and agree, "School sucks!" They'll be surprised at your response and that you understand what they're going through (even though they still have to finish their homework).

- Gain a sense of humor. Sometimes children need to know from their parent(s) that a low grade on an assignment or test is not the end of the world. (Blame it on the moon's gravity).

- Children should know that no matter what others may say, their school grades do not define them as a person.

- Sleep in. Turn off the alarm clock. Don't plan an outing. Stay in your pajamas. Watch movies or play board games. Take a nap with the family pet. Do nothing and decompress. Nothing else matters.

- Identify "family" hidden talents—the quirkier the better—by researching genealogy, history, mystery, fable and country origin. This helps children build their own identity.

- Expose your children to entrepreneurship. Get them involved in their own "start-up" project. Brainstorm on what they are passionate about and help them make it a reality. New ideas can sometimes turn into lifetime successes.

- Exercise "flexible thinking." Take the "bird's-eye view" approach when listening to your child's point of view on issues that are important to your child. Flexible thinking elevates understanding, comprehension and visualization—helpful tools during academic learning.

- Be careful when critiquing your child's homework. As long as the words on a page continue to flow, then poor spelling, repetitive sentences or incorrect grammar can all be fixed later with an eraser and teacher help.

- Appreciate the moments watching your child daydream. This is where positive experiences of the past are relived and new experiences are yet to be explored.

School is important, but without first knowing how children learn, parents and educators will never fully understand or appreciate their abilities.

Brandon age 7

"Smile. It makes people wonder
what you are thinking about."

-Lorraine Donovan
Author

CHAPTER 56

Keeping the Conversation Going

Some parents are unsure as to whether they should inform their child as to the results of an academic evaluation. And it doesn't help when someone providing the evaluation delivers the findings in a whisper, "Your child has dyslexia" (aka specific learning disability).

A child or adult who has dyslexia needs to own it! Hiding a learning disability from a child who struggles in school, powerless to do anything about it, is not an acceptable alternative.

Children are resilient. They're also smart, compassionate, understanding and loving. They deserve to be involved in their emotional and physical well-being. Children can also provide great insight into how they prefer to learn.

It isn't necessary to go it alone. There are millions of like-minded dyslexics, of all ages, who are proud to be part of a very special community of people who think and learn differently. The key is to focus on the positive, accentuating one's strengths and embracing new ways to navigate and advocate one's dyslexia style of learning.

Saying "I'm dyslexic and proud of it!" can be incredibly freeing. And for those who cock their head and seem confused by what was just said, just smile at them. Maybe, just maybe, they'll get it and smile back....

A CHILD'S TOUCHSTONE

Index

CRIME: 346, 360

CROWDING: 22-23

DAYDREAM: 213, 383

DEATH: 347

DECODE A WORD: 10, 17

DECODING: 8, 17, 28, 56, 150, 219, 227, 300

DECODING OF LANGUAGE: 8, 28

DEFICITS IN MEMORY: 13

DELAY TACTICS: 173, 175, 177, 179, 181, 183

DENIAL: 151, 193

DEPRESSION: 43, 53, 84, 341-342, 355, 372

DETECTING THE SYMPTOMS: 19, 21, 23, 25

DIAGNOSIS: 31, 146, 149, 156, 179, 296, 359

DIFFICULTY REMEMBERING: 29-30, 36, 52, 213, 241

DISABILITY: 7, 9-10, 13-14, 19, 28, 43, 47-49, 87-89, 91, 94-95, 127-128, 130, 145, 147, 149-150, 152, 155-156, 159, 169-171, 173-175, 177-179, 181-182, 198, 205, 253, 277, 295, 299, 329, 333, 337, 347, 353, 355-359, 361, 363, 365, 367, 369, 371-373, 375, 385

DISABILITY CATEGORIES: 13

DISABILITY HARASSMENT: 353, 355, 357, 359, 361, 363, 365, 367, 369, 371, 373, 375

DISCRIMINATION: 80, 84, 94, 123, 201, 356, 365, 375

DISTRACTED: 21-22, 80, 84, 204, 319

DISTRACTIBILITY: 21, 85

DOUBLE DEFICIT: 17

WORKING MEMORY: 14, 17, 20-22, 29, 35-36, 41, 48-49, 56, 91-93, 102, 160, 207, 212, 214, 217, 227, 255, 261, 265, 299

WORKSHEET(S): 97-98, 127

WRITING: 8, 10, 13-16, 23-24, 28, 35, 40, 44, 49, 55-56, 75-76, 122, 130, 146, 160, 193-194, 213, 227, 237-238, 247, 250, 257, 261, 281, 291-292, 300, 303, 305, 312, 315-316, 326, 372, 375

WRITTEN EXPRESSION: 14, 53, 91, 93, 97-98, 122, 128, 130, 300

WRITTEN LANGUAGE: 13, 95, 149, 299